PENGUIN

BRIT-THINK
AMERI-THINK

Jane Walmsley was born in New York, but has lived in England for more than twelve years, where she works as a television broadcaster and journalist. She is married to a Brit, who is undoubtedly the source of much of her insight into the British character. She and her husband have one daughter.

BRIT-
THINK

AMERI-
THINK

A TRANSATLANTIC SURVIVAL GUIDE

JANE WALMSLEY

with cartoons by Gray Jolliffe

PENGUIN BOOKS

PENGUIN BOOKS
Published by the Penguin Group
Viking Penguin, a division of Penguin Books USA Inc.,
375 Hudson Street, New York, New York 10014, U.S.A.
Penguin Books Ltd, 27 Wrights Lane,
London W8 5TZ, England
Penguin Books Australia Ltd, Ringwood,
Victoria, Australia
Penguin Books Canada Ltd, 10 Alcorn Avenue, Suite 300,
Toronto, Ontario, Canada M4V 3B2
Penguin Books (N.Z.) Ltd, 182–190 Wairau Road,
Auckland 10, New Zealand

Penguin Books Ltd. Registered Offices:
Harmondsworth, Middlesex, England

First published in Great Britain by Harrap Ltd., 1986
This revised edition first published in the United States of America in
Penguin Books 1987
Published simultaneously in Canada

7   9   10   8   6

Copyright © Jane Walmsley, 1986, 1987
All rights reserved

ISBN 0 14 00.9367 2
(CIP data available)

Grateful acknowledgment is made for permission to reproduce the illustrations
by Gray Jolliffe. Illustrations © Gray Jolliffe, 1986. Reproduced with the
permission of Harrap Ltd., U.K.

Printed in the United States of America
Set in Garamond
Designed by Mary A. Wirth

To my daughter Katie . . .
who has an American mother
and a British father, and is
—as she puts it—"haff and hawf."

In writing this book, I've tried hard to be evenhanded, and fair to both sides. If there's someone I haven't insulted . . . I'm sorry.

CONTENTS

PREFACE

I came to Britain as a college student in the early seventies, married a Londoner, and have lived here since . . . but there are still days when I feel like a war bride who travelled in the wrong direction. "Why's that," gasp astonished Yank friends, "when London is so *civilised?*" (A sure sign that they have visited Harrods' food halls.)

I admit my feelings are most pronounced in mid-winter, when British central heating fails to function, and resident Yanks die of exposure indoors—but this is a detail. The longer I stay, the more aware I become that we are very different peoples, grown far apart since 1776. I submit that the so-called special relationship between Britain and America is now one part history, and one part wishful thinking. Sure, Yanks love London, and Brits watch *Dynasty,* and everybody eats at McDonald's, but that's not the point. We have developed separate attitudes and aspirations, which I classify as *Brit-think* and *Ameri-think.*

During my fifteen years here, Anglo-American relations have weathered several storms. There was the controversial deployment of U.S. cruise missiles in Britain, the 1985 collapse of the pound against the dollar, and—more recently—the flap about letting American F-111's zap Tripoli from British bases. Not surprisingly, all this has led to a certain amount of transatlantic tension and misunderstanding.

More and more, I find myself acting as a kind of interpreter for friends from both sides of the pond. Their general confusion manifests itself in specifics (Yanks on Brits): "What, *no* late-night TV? These guys *trying* to lose money?" or (Brits on Yanks): "Do they really need to mutilate the carbons every time they use a credit card?"

What both sides *really* fail to understand are the basics—the cultural themes, the habits of mind which determine the way the other guys behave. In order that I may never again have to explain why Brits form orderly queues, or why Yanks insist that you "have a nice day" whether you want one or not, I have written *Brit-Think, Ameri-Think*. I hope that no one will leave home without it.

BRIT-
THINK

AMERI-
THINK

1

FIRST THINGS FIRST

THE *LANGUAGE* OF ANGLO-AMERI-THINK

Confused? You won't be. Just remember that:

UK		US
chips	=	french fries
crisps	=	potato chips
biscuit	=	cookie or cracker
scone	=	biscuit (baking powder)
crumpet	=	UNKNOWN
UNKNOWN	=	English muffin
tart	=	hooker
ground floor	=	first floor
first floor	=	second floor
vest	=	undershirt
waistcoat	=	vest
knickers	=	underpants
knickerbockers	=	knickers
lorry	=	truck
van	=	pickup
juggernaut	=	big (mother) truck
pickup	=	hooker
fag	=	cigarette
poof	=	fag
wally	=	jerk
jerk	=	off

. . . and so on. But translating words and phrases is the easy part. It takes years of Anglo-Amerexperience to understand *the thinking behind them* . . . and that's the hard part.

George Bernard Shaw said it best, though many have said it badly ever since. America and Britain are two nations divided by a common language. Between us is a Great Philosophical and Cultural Divide, which is obscured by the familiar lingo. Our respective heads of government may burble on about "common bonds" and "special relationships"—but the truth is that, in the eighties, Brit-think and Ameri-think are lightyears apart. We cherish widely different values and aspirations, and have developed separate habits of mind. Only the names remain the same . . . and there's some doubt about those. In some ways, a camel and a porpoise have more in common.

That's the bad news. But, dedicated travelers and internationalists take heart. The *good* news is that—with no language barrier to overcome—you've a once-in-a-lifetime opportunity to penetrate a foreign mind. So, if you've been perplexed by the transatlantic psycho-gap, and feel that your holidays (or business dealings) will be enhanced if only you can bridge it, then here's a guide to basic Brit-think and Ameri-think. Mind-reading for the jetset.

BASIC BRIT-THINK AND AMERI-THINK: THE MOST IMPORTANT THINGS TO KNOW

1. I'M GONNA LIVE FOREVER

—————— A M E R I - T H I N K ——————

The single most important thing to know about Americans—the attitude which *truly* distinguishes them from the British, and explains much superficially odd behavior—is that *Americans think that death is optional.* They may not admit it, and will probably laugh if it's suggested; but it's a state of mind—a kind of national leitmotiv if you like—that colors everything they do. There's a nagging suspicion that you can delay death (or—who knows?—avoid it altogether) if you really try. This explains the common preoccupation with health, aerobics, prune juice, plastic surgery, and education.

The idea is that you're given one life to live, and it's up to you to get it right. You should:

- use the time to maximize individual potential (have a nose job, get a college degree) so as to ensure the highest-quality life possible.
- take care of your body so it will last. If extended life span —or even immortality—proves possible, at least you're ready.

That's the secret of America's fundamental optimism; but it's not as cheery as it sounds. It imposes on the individual a whole range of duties and responsibilities. Your life is in your own hands . . . and the quality of that life as well. You owe it to yourself to be beautiful, clever, skinny, successful, and healthy. If you fail, it's because you're not trying hard enough . . . (you didn't jog regularly, you should've eaten more bran). Death becomes your fault.

—————————— B R I T - T H I N K ——————————

Brit-think on the subject is fundamentally different, and accounts for the yawning gulf in national attitudes. Brits keep a weather eye on the Sword of Damocles, suspended above their heads. Lives are to be lived with a certain detachment, and a sense of distance preserved. One rolls with the punches. It's fruitless to try to take control, bad form to get too involved, arrogant and self-important to attempt to outwit destiny.

Events must be allowed to run their natural course. Stay cool, and *never* be seen to try too hard (Americans are so intense!) since anyone with half a brain should recognize the central absurdity of existence (Monty Python was so apt) and accept the inevitable. Success—if it's to count—must appear effort less. Since nothing matters very much anyway, think twice before making important sacrifices. Never run for a bus. Never skip tea.

2. NEW IS GOOD

—————————— A M E R I - T H I N K ——————————

Meet an American for the first time, and he's likely to greet you with, "So, what's new?" (abridged in Manhattan to "So, new?"). He wants more than a general progress report. One small part of him means it literally, begging an answer like, "Well, I've got a new Chevy/lover/food processor." Because in America, *new* is *good*. Americans are the world's greatest believers in progress. Life gets better all the time—or should. They expect a seventy-year crescendo, starting at not-so-hot, and rising to terrific.

Nothing will convince a True American (even an elderly one) that "things were better 'way back when.'" They point in evidence at the history of modern medicine: once there was smallpox, now there isn't. Old things can be treated with a certain irreverence, since something better is always just around the corner. *America* is still new—still warm and gently throbbing—and so are the most desirable things in it. Over much of the country new property attracts a higher price than old, new shopping malls snatch customers from "old" haunts as soon as they cut the ribbon on the parking lot. New products are greeted with enthusiasm, since advanced versions always include "improvements." No point in clinging grimly to the past, or we'd never have traded gramophones for color TVs, buckshot for Star Wars, or headaches for coated aspirin.

—————————— B R I T - T H I N K ——————————

Life—and the simple passage of time—does *not* presuppose progress. At best, there are large flat areas. There's little proof that things get better, and a great deal of evidence to suggest the opposite. Look at defense: we live with the threat of the Big Bang. Look at architecture: Victorians built better houses than we do. Look at world affairs: we have to waste time listening to the ravings of Muslim lunatics. Look at sportsmanship: it was fairer play before they invented steroids. Look at AIDS. That's new.

True Brits loathe newness, and display a profound fear of change. They see modern life as increasingly uncertain, events as random, and "untried" ideas as undesirable. Even small changes can cause Brit-trauma, with the nation shaken to its roots at suggestions that traditional red phone boxes may be painted yellow. Far better to preserve the status quo, to hope that custom and ritual will somehow counter the capriciousness of fate. (Britain is the heartland of "We've Always Done It This Way.") Conclusion: change nothing unless forced. Remember that God usually gets it right the first time.

3. NEVER FORGET YOU'VE GOT A CHOICE

——————— A M E R I - T H I N K ——————

Choice—lots of it—is as dear to the American heart as newness. The point about choice is to exercise it as much as possible. That's why Yanks *elect* so many people: presidents, governors, judges, senators, congressmen, and dogcatchers.

Americans never commit themselves to anything for life. Leaders you can't change—like monarchs—make them nervous. They reserve the right to review decisions periodically; anything less is an attack on personal freedom, and reminds them of Communism. They even get edgy when fruit they like is out of season. Limited choice makes them think of Moscow matrons queuing hopelessly for goods. Nowhere do people view restrictions with more alarm. They mistrust package holidays and long-term investments. Contracts of employment must contain appropriate "get out" clauses. They plan vacations and shop for Christmas at the last minute, and make final decisions only when they've considered all possible choices. They conduct business by phone, and avoid committing anything to paper. They don't even like restaurants with set menus. The right to substitute a tossed salad for french fries is enshrined in the Constitution. Americans like to live life à la carte.

. . .

The range of personal choice must be strictly limited. (This is reflected in the retail industry, where dresses come in four sizes, shoes in one width, and ice cream in three flavors.) Too many options only confuse people, and encourage them to behave in a greedy and selfish way. It's part of human nature to be happier when our horizons are limited, someone else is in charge, and we know what's expected of us. That's why monarchs are so useful, and the class system survives. It's also why we enjoyed such widespread national contentment during the Second World War. All you had to know was how many coupons were left in your ration book. All appearances to the contrary, the heat was off.

Since then, the argument goes, it's been downhill all the way. More options and higher expectations have spawned the "Me" generation, which doesn't understand the relationship between virtue and restriction. It'll end in tears or *anarchy* (which is British for "unlimited choice").

4. SMART MONEY

Choice is the same thing as freedom, which is the same thing as money, and that's the real secret of the national fondness for cash. It's not that Americans are by nature greedier or more acquisitive than their European counterparts. They're no fonder of their dishwashers and microwaves than the British of their color TVs and double glazing . . . no happier with their automatic orange-juicers and garbage compacters in Houston than a Liverpool housewife with a toasted sandwich–maker or a duvet. Nor do Pennsylvania steelworkers push harder for wage settlements than Yorkshire miners. It's just that Americans admire money more openly. They see it as a measure of success, and the final guarantee of personal choice. In short, Money is Power—and power is a good thing. Lack of power makes you a Shlep. Money is a hedge against Shlephood.

Furthermore, you *can* take it with you—or, if you've got enough, you may not have to go. Cash gives room for maneuver. If it turns out that death *is* optional—or science comes up with a commercial miracle—your dollars guarantee that you won't be ignored. Money buys the best . . . and the best is your birthright.

The public stance of the middle-to-upper classes is to pooh-pooh money ("not my first priority") and instead to speak passionately of "the quality of life." By this, Brits mean things spiritual or cultural, which—they maintain—have nothing to do with hard cash. The price of theater tickets notwithstanding.

The theory is that money can't buy taste, or style, or a sense of priorities—which are things you're born with. (Wealthy people are born with more than poor ones.) Your spending habits are seen as a reflection of breeding and the quality of your mind, and allow others to make judgments about your background and personal style. Haggling about money is okay for miners and steelworkers (just). Others should concern themselves with loyalty to employers, or duty to the wider community. It is the custom of the wealthiest Brits (Captains of Industry and/or Royals) to periodically remind the masses of the virtues of self-denial and restraint. This is called *noblesse oblige.*

The single-minded pursuit of ready cash is simply vulgar, and undermines the human spirit. Of course, you've got to *have* money—because penury is unbecoming, and gets in the way. But enough is enough. After all—you can't take it with you. Americans never understand that.

5. THE CONSENSUS SOCIETY

AMERI-THINK

Yup, that's what they call it. What they mean is that virtually everyone in America—be he farmer, welder, or Wall Street wizard—wants the same thing. Their separate definitions of "the good life," if you asked them, would be amazingly similar. Nor do any of them—regardless of financial position—tend to question the fundamental social order. With the exception of a few aging refugees from Haight-Ashbury, America in the eighties is sure it's got it right. The nation's politics reflect this. There's not much ideological distance between the two major parties. Sure, the Republicans are supposed to favor Big Business, lower taxes, and centralized government, while Democrats are traditionally more liberal, freer public spenders, and happier to devolve decisions. But they're all after the same *result*—a strong, secure, and unabashedly capitalist America.

BRIT-THINK

Politics in Britain is a civil war without weapons. Even elections do not buy us a period of peace and quiet—the losers will not accept the result.

Brian Walden
London Standard

Of course they won't, when whole sections of the community see their personal interests as irrevocably bound up in the fortunes of one particular party. It's a war all right, between the "them" side and the "us" side, and it's a fight to the death. No chance of defeat with honor; no reconciliation; no magnanimity. The winner takes all, and the loser retires to sulk in a corner for four or five years.

You don't *choose* your side of the body politic; you're born there. To break away represents a betrayal of class and family. Your Party Is You, and vice versa. It is on your side, even when it is wrecking your prospects and the economy of the nation. To Brits, party loyalty has nothing to do with pragmatism, and abject failure is no good reason for desertion. No: Brit-politics are not really about personal *gain*. They are about class dominance and principles. Compromise with the Other Side is dangerous, since it blunts the cutting edge of despair. Cooperation . . . what's that? This is why Brits conclude that all forms of progress are impossible. They are right. Under the present system, nothing moves.

6. *"ME-THINK" VS. "WE-THINK"*

——————— A M E R I - T H I N K ———————

"*Moi*—I come first." Miss Piggy said it, and touched a chord deep in the hearts of her countrymen. An American considers that his first duty and obligation is to look after Number One. This follows from "I'm gonna live forever," because it stands to reason that you've got to take care of yourself if you're going to last. If each person concentrates on attaining his "personal best" —and achieves inner fulfillment—we will have created a better society.

Without knowing it, most Yanks support the ideas of Adam Smith, the economist who advanced the theory that the individual working in his own interests leads ultimately to the greatest good of the state. A strong society is merely the sum of strong parts. It's often said that America is the heartland of individualism . . . and this is what people mean. You protect your own interests by making choices—lots of them. If you've acquired money—which gives you more leverage—then so much the better. It is no accident that Frank Sinatra scored a monster hit with "I Did It My Way." Frankie understands "Me-think."

"Piggy-think" does not sit easily with Brits. It strikes them as selfish, and a bit brutal. Whether they vote Tory or Labour, they've spent years living under various permutations of socialist government. This has created different habits of mind, and softened the collective rhetoric. *"Moi*—I come first" sticks in the throat. Brits of most persuasions are happiest talking about "self-reliance" and "the common good," which reminds them of the War, the Crown, and the BBC in no particular order. This has a great deal of social credibility, but—paradoxically—often turns out to mean "my right to do what's best for me, and hope that your requirements don't get in the way."

Culturally, socially, psychologically, *literally*—Brits form orderly queues. They like to keep things nice and cozy. Fundamental to "we-think" is the dread of inciting a contest—a scrum. Brits are by nature reluctant to throw down the gauntlet; and "I come first" is a challenge to others—notification of battle. Strong stuff, where there are winners and losers, and the weak go to the wall. Once the gloves are off, no one can predict the outcome.

This carries with it the risk of change, bloodletting, and general social turbulence. (No shakeups, please—we're British.) "We-think" creates the impression of a kind, more caring society, where rich and poor alike are cushioned against the harsh realities of unbridled competition. One can't win by much, or lose by much. So goes the Brit-myth.

2

BRITS AND YANKS ABROAD . . . BUSINESS AND PLEASURE

A M E R I - S T Y L E

Generally speaking, Yanks abroad come in two varieties: groomed and casual. Age has little to do with categories, since you can fit into either at sixteen or seventy. Geriatrics in stretch denims are not uncommon. Neither are six-year-olds in fur coats.

Commonly, the American traveling abroad for pleasure is casual, but *equipped.* He's got the most expensive "walking shoes" money can buy, and these are hideously ugly but orthopedically correct. His wardrobe is largely composed of crush-proof petroleum by-products. He has nylon-coated rainwear and fold-away hats, collapsible umbrellas and lightweight high-resolution sound videocameras. There's a pocket calculator to work out his restaurant tips, convert pounds into piastres or kilograms, wake him in the morning, and deliver regular updates on the New York Stock Exchange. He has brought with him a battery-powered toothbrush, an electrical converter, and matching Water Pik. He's got a separate case for double quantities of all vital medications and a spare pair of soft lenses, plus a container of dental floss in case the Water Pik breaks down.

· · ·

AMER-EXECUTIVE

When traveling abroad, he is groomed to corporate perfection. He is careful to look prosperous, heterosexual, and clean. His fingernails are immaculate as a dentist's, and beautifully buffed. He appears to believe that many an important business deal rides on the quality of his manicure.

He wears the statutory Burberry raincoat-with-plaid-lining over his four-hundred-dollar suit, which may have a matching vest, but is in any case a nice mid-gray pinstripe or herringbone from Brooks Brothers or Saks. It fits perfectly on the shoulders.

His hair is as neat as his nails. If it's thick enough, he wears it cut like JFK's; if there's gray at the temples, he leans toward Blake Carrington. He hopes to look like a Kennedy-clone, or at least a graduate of Harvard Business School. In fact, he's been to Syracuse or Ohio U . . . or (if over 45) maybe nowhere.

Wristwatches are important. He prefers tasteful traditional with lizard strap, or Cartier tank (the gen. article). Above all, no lumpy chronometers. His briefcase is fine calfskin, unscathed by

I'm off to England on Friday. Remind me to turn my watch back five hundred years.

the journey through three different airports (when traveling, he slips it inside a protective drawstring cover).

He is the living incarnation of that popular East Coast adage, "Dress British, think Yiddish." He knows that Yanks are perceived abroad as garish and tasteless dressers, and wants to avert the charge. There's not a thread of Madras plaid, or polyester, or Ultra-Suede in his Louis Vuitton luggage. He's purchased with care, to appear understated but unmistakably prominent. He doesn't understand that *British* for understated but unmistakably prominent is SCRUFFY (as in the Chancellor of the Exchequer's briefcase).

AMERI-WIFE

Her role models are drawn from *Dallas* and *Dynasty.* She sees herself as the "new woman," peddled constantly on the covers of *Vogue* and *Good Housekeeping.* She knows you can BE FABULOUS AT 40, TURN HEADS AT 50. Look at Raquel and Jane. Look at Joan and Sophia. Look at Sue Ellen.

For the past two weeks, Ameri-wife has doubled up on her California stretch classes and tennis lessons back home in Houston, in preparation for her trip. She shed a few pounds for Europe, so as to indulge in pasta and croissants with a free mind. But each time she eats, her waistbands get tighter, and—unable to convert stones to pounds—she longs for the reassurance of her digital bathroom scale. Already, she's liberated the laxatives from her husband's "medications" suitcase, and is preoccupied with regularity (Europeans should eat more fiber).

Wardrobe includes pastel-colored jumpsuits and matching Nike sports shoes for sightseeing, with plenty of chunky gold jewelry. (Loves "anything deco.") Hair is the blond-streaked mane of a Texas lioness, a bit long for her age, but "look at Dyan Cannon." Anyway, "he won't let me cut it!"

Ameri-wife enthuses a great deal about visiting ancient sites, museums, and theaters, but what she's really looking forward to in London is a chance to *shop.* She'll buy more place settings of her favorite Staffordshire dinner service, and some Waterford crystal—"so much cheaper than in Houston." She'll stock up on cashmeres, Boots mascara, and anything Burberry. Then, if there's time left, she'll spend it looking for "cute places to have lunch." (See The Importance of Being "Cute," p. 41)

A BRIT GOES STATESIDE

———————— B R I T - S T Y L E ————————

He is somehow the antithesis of the Somerset Maugham figure: the man decked out in a tropical cream-colored suit with matching fedora, languorously sipping mint tea under whirling ceiling fans and avoiding mad dogs and the noonday sun. It seems that, when the Empire struck back, the Brit-sense of tropical attire took a direct hit.

America in summer can be a hot place, and the visiting Brit often exudes discomfort. He looks a bit frayed at the edges, and generally is as *under* equipped as his American counterpart is *over*. This has nothing to do with income group. It is a policy decision. So, he does not have the converter and the Water Pik. He does not even have much of a toothbrush. He's purchased no extra clothes for the journey, and the ones he has make no concession to the climate . . . "no point, when I'll only be there for a week or two." He is "making do" by wearing the trousers to an old office suit, teamed with a short-sleeved Aertex shirt. It has a cream background (he dislikes the "glare" of pure white) and has a way of looking soiled in strong sunlight.

Feet are clad in dark City slip-ons, because the only casual shoes he owns are Wellingtons ("for the gardening"), some old cricket shoes, and bedroom slippers. If caught short, he'll splash out in a pair of rubber foam flip-flops halfway through the vacation, but only after he's been forced to wear his City slip-ons down to the beach.

The sun presents real problems; he burns if he stands for too long under a strong light bulb. So he wears lots of protective cream (his one item of special expenditure) and always needs help in applying it to his back. He discovers that his bathing trunks are revealing by American standards. (Yanks consider anything skimpier than boxer shorts as *de facto* flashing.) He has *not* bought a matching cover-up (*de rigueur* by U.S. pools) and appears every day sporting yesterday's Aertex, unbuttoned to the waist to reveal gradually reddening chest. He has *not* invested in swishy sunglasses ("£30 for *those*?") and instead has shades that clip on over his prescription glasses. For some reason, he usually wears them flipped *up*.

MRS. BRIT

So does his wife. If she is middle-aged, she is his counterpart—but slightly better equipped. For instance, she has sandals. They're robust, tannish leather flatties with lots of buckles to adjust the width, and owe more to Dr. Scholl than to high fashion. But they are comfy, especially as her ankles tend to swell and she "retains water in hot climates" (anything with temperatures higher than Reykjavik). She never quite gets to grips with tropical sun colors ("too garish, like Hawaiian shirts") and instead favors subdued shades of sage green to gray . . . "more tasteful and flattering." Cream is nice, especially with sage green, avocado, or brown (or all together). At heart, she is happiest wearing the colors she's used in the living room.

She worries excessively about *food* . . . not about gaining weight, or cholesterol, or regularity, but about getting "gyppy tummy" (the runs). She worries even in "sanitary" countries like the U.S., and has strange theories about what causes it ("raw onion with hamburger, too much ice in drinks, air conditioning everywhere, even in cars"). She doesn't care for the tea, the coffee, the cooking, or the salad dressing, is iffy about the bread ("What's a bagel?") but approves of the variety of fresh produce ("The quality is nice . . . such a good seasonal selection!").

BRIT GROOVERETTE

The younger woman has her act together, sartorially at least. She's bought playsuits in pastel crushed cottons, and sexy off-the-shoulder T-shirts for the discos (except that at American resorts she can't find many, so repairs often to the local hamburger-and-singles bar). Her accent is a godsend, and for the first time in her life she's told it's "gorgeous"—even if she comes from Liverpool or Birmingham. She finds that a grooverette's reputation for sexual rapacity precedes her (somehow borne out by her pink-tipped, wet-gelled hair and selection of earrings hanging from one multiply pierced lobe).

In truth, she's something of an innocent abroad, never having been far out of Mum's earshot. But she enjoys her notoriety and laughs a lot, and likes being teased even when she doesn't understand the jokes. People always say she's "so cute" when she says "chips" instead of french fries. (See The Importance of Being

---

U.S./U.K. GUIDE: WHAT NOT TO DO IN EACH OTHER'S COUNTRIES

Ameri-Gaffes
When in the U.K., don't:

1. Buy china and Waterford crystal, then speak obsessively of the shipping charges for sending it home.
2. Buy cashmere. Especially boring classics that are only five dollars more in Macy's.
3. Buy tartans, or wear tartan berets in the streets because it makes you "feel British." Don't go into shops and insist on looking for your family tartan, especially if your name is Yablonsky.
4. Talk about genealogy . . . yours or other people's. No one cares. You and everyone else you will meet are probably seven billionth in line for the British throne. This is especially true if you are of Armenian descent.
5. Talk about how "civilized" London is. It isn't.
6. Forget to stand on the right of escalators in subways. It irritates natives.
7. Be sycophantically complimentary about members of the Royal Family. It's creepy.
8. Assume that people you meet would secretly like to trade places with you. They wouldn't. They like being British.

"Cute," p. 41.) She doesn't mind the food because she rarely eats it, sticking mainly to a liquid diet. Cocktails. It's the best summer holiday she's ever had. She just can't get over the thrilling idea that when you date waiters in America, you date Americans.

Brit-Blunders
When in the U.S., don't:

1. Eat hamburgers or sandwiches with a knife and fork. Even if they're huge and sloppy.
2. Wear ankle socks with sandals. Unless they're Day-Glo pink, and you're under twenty-five.
3. Insist that you eat ice cream only in hot weather. Ice cream is America's national dish. Temperature has nothing to do with it.
4. Complain about the ubiquitous air conditioning. (Take your cardigan to restaurants and in cars.) Do not try to open the windows in skyscrapers for "fresh air." Ameri-windows do not open; Yanks prefer a "controlled environment."
5. Remove the ice from drinks, or ask the waitress to leave it out so that you get more Coca-Cola in the glass for your money.
6. Be insulting about American television. You're already watching most of it at home.
7. Wonder aloud how all the sunny days will affect plants (they have sprinkler systems) or how people get by without better public transport (they have cars).
8. Call dessert "pudding" . . . "What's for pudding?" They won't understand, and they'll think *you're* one.

3

STRICTLY BUSINESS

What George Bernard Shaw once said about men and women could apply equally well to British and American businessmen: "They're destined never to understand each other, but doomed to forever try." Take the hungry and hopeful Yank, resplendent in his flawless suit and matching manicure. He has failed to hoist one important psychological point, and it will prove his undoing: Brits are perverse, and respond badly to personal packaging. Perfect grooming strikes them as suspicious . . . slightly intimidating. They become wary of manipulation, and hence resistant to propositions. It is hard to trust someone who looks richer than you feel.

Corporate Yank who wants to start a productive dialogue must try to appear sympathetic. This means *human,* and even (here he'll have to work against the grain) *flawed.* OUT with zomboid corporate-speak. ELIMINATE phrases like "In Chicago, we're very excited about the new data-control operation . . . , which sound nearly as plastic as "Have a nice day," and make Brit-eyes glaze over. Hair can be rumpled, shoes a bit scuffed. Suit should look lived in.

This is a hard lesson for Yanks to learn. Usual U.S. business practice dictates that those trying to clinch deals must convey—in dress and demeanor—the impression that

1. they have made money, and are therefore at ease with it, and
2. they treat it Very Seriously. Nothing on this planet is more important than The Deal.

There will be no sloppy mistakes. Perfect attire reassures others that you are equally immaculate in your thinking. (You have covered every wrinkle.)

It is not unknown for Brit associates to maroon a Yank in this very professionalism. It's a form of intellectual one-upmanship to suggest that "of course it's important, Old Chap, but there's more to life than the bottom line." There is, for example, the countryside, and Sunday lunch. Corporate Brit can't resist pricking the bubble of gung-ho–ness. It's a nasty trick, and visiting Yank reports back to Chicago that "you can't talk to these people."

The thing Brits hate most in Yank associates is their infernal *optimism*. This reads to them as the worst kind of naïveté. Brits often cultivate, for business purposes, the image of those who are world-weary with experience, and have been around all the houses at least once. There is a common reluctance to entertain new ideas, make special efforts, or ever miss the 5:46 home to Weybridge. Instead, one earns corporate Brownie points for "making the best of a bad job."

Enter the fresh-faced Yank, brimming with enthusiasm and fiscal fitness. The Irresistible Force has met the Immovable Object. He's reinvented the wheel, and seems bent on talking about it. He comes on like a corporate adolescent as he babbles about "more cost-effective ways," and "simpler solutions." Brits have mixed emotions when these appear to work.

SUCCEEDING IN BUSINESS

——————— B R I T - T H I N K ———————

A nation of shopkeepers it may be, but in the final analysis, Brits and business are spiritually incompatible. "Business" is all about meeting the changing needs of consumers, and Brits loathe change. They especially hate *consumer-led* change, believing that the little sods ought to take what they can get and like it. Fortunately, British consumers are docile, not to say supine. They do not demand a liberal returns policy in stores, and therefore are stuck with all purchases unless faulty. They will eat food in any combination preordained by restaurants. They will accept prescriptions from doctors without asking simple questions about contents or side effects, and—if damaged—will not sue. If they buy goods which break within short periods (the blade snaps on an electric blender, the washing machine floods, the heel comes off a shoe), they will accept blame for having misused it. They are content to purchase all electrical appliances *minus* the plugs, thus involving themselves in extra expense and inconvenience.

The result is that British businessmen are drunk with power, and never give the suckers an even break. For years they have sold people ovens too small to cook a big turkey in, twin-tub "automatic" washers which will not launder clothes without human intervention, refrigerators which require primitive defrosting methods, and teensy expensive sandwiches—which would not satisfy an anorexic in the last stages of decline.

Not surprisingly, British industry is—by American standards —shrouded in secrecy. For instance, it often displays a deeprooted fear of the press. It seems that British businessmen can't bear the idea of being *watched* while doing whatever it is that they do. This is probably because they can't *explain* whatever it is that they do . . . except to say, "We've always done it this way."

INTIMIDATION AND DESKS

———————— A M E R I - T H I N K ————————

The American office desk is a symbol of status and power, as is the waiting time you—the supplicant—spend in the outer office before you *see* the desk. (NOTE: In Los Angeles—and especially in the film and television industry—a special formula applies, wherein the relative importance of the executive you're about to see is inversely proportional to the waiting time you spend in his outer office, and to his height—i.e., a two-hour wait should produce a man who is both impotent and short.)

However: the more senior the executive, the larger his desk; so, Big Boss will sit behind a surface that a family of ten could live on for a year. Unless it's roughly the size of a platform at a Calcutta railway station, it doesn't count. The point is that desks are macho, and desks intimidate. They also protect . . . interposing a beautifully grained and polished fortress between Big Boss and you.

You are placed at an instant disadvantage. First, you will have to shout across vast spaces in order to be heard. Big Boss will also ensure that your guest chair is low, and the desk rim level with your mouth. This gives him a chance to say, "What? Can you speak up? I can't hear!" until you are thoroughly rattled. Second —and most important—it places you too far away to judge whether Big Boss is stupid or smart. If he is seated behind his desk when you come in, you won't know if he's tall or short. Or thin or fat. You will not spot his contact lenses or recent hair implant. Or the fact that he's just had the bags beneath his eyes done.

The large desk will be housed in an equally impressive office, with breathtaking panoramas of city skyline beyond slimline venetian blinds, over shaded landscapes of plush carpet. It should look like J. R. Ewing's office, presided over by a Barbie Doll secretary who is also an acolyte. Already it's two against one.

─────────────── B R I T - T H I N K ───────────────

Brit executives understand intimidation, too, but their style is somewhat different. Surprisingly, senior men—especially in the upper echelons of government and broadcasting—have scruffy offices with half-dead plants producing mutant stems on dusty window sills. They bend over desks which appear to have been bought secondhand at an industrial closeout. The phones have dials, the typewriters are antiques, and so are some of the secretaries. The tea lady shrieks, "Tea, dear?" from the corridor each time she passes, and sloshes stewed brew into half-melted plastic cups. "That'll be 7p, dear."

In short, Brit-boss lacks glossy props. But (and this is important) he is on his Own Turf. Despite the seediness of the sur-

roundings—or perhaps because of them—he hopes to project a sense of class . . . superior intellect, breeding, and education, which—as every Brit knows—are perfectly consistent with being down at the heels. Brit-boss has also been brought up to believe that a man in command can afford to underplay his hand.

Unfortunately, the pitch works only on other Brits. Visiting Yanks are not sufficiently conversant with the subtleties of the class system to be impressed. What they see merely confuses them. They do not think about Oxbridge or the Corridors of Power or the Old Boys' Net. They simply return to the hotel and wonder why such a Big Cheese looks like a real Shlep.

4

BRITS AND YANKS
AT HOME

HOME AS BACKDROP

AMERI-THINK

The home is the ultimate expression of Me. It is one area over
which an American insists on perfect control; a place to display
aspirations and live out fantasies . . . however eclectic these may
be. Home is multifaceted Me.

There's a "tropical" room with whirling ceiling fans and
plenty of rattan; an English Tudor dining room with hammered
beams in the ceiling; an apricot-and-gilt bedroom where one can
indulge a taste for Louis XVI; and a hi-tech post-modernist media
room with faux-marbled walls. What matter if the exterior is red
brick neo-Federalist, or Cape Cod shingle? If America is a cultural melting pot, so is its domestic architecture . . . as a quick drive
through Beverly Hills will confirm. Forget consistency. It's *impact* we're after.

Members of the aspirational middle classes will have an interior decorator as surely as they will have hairdressers, gynecolo-
gists, and cleaning ladies. The role of the decorator is not to
"impose" taste (surely not), but to "interpret" the client's *life-
style*. Ameri-clients will gladly pay the heftiest fees in return for
the assurance that they *have* lifestyles.

A good decorator can do much to mask personal shortcomings. Shaky taste can be "re-edited" into something acceptable;
even a client who is a real slob can be cunningly repackaged as

"California casual." This means lots of scatter cushions on the floor and Navajo blankets thrown casually over the backs of chairs so the mess looks intentional.

Yanks enjoy creating domestic scenarios ("home as backdrop") and are accustomed to shelling out proportionately. Five thousand dollars per room, counting furniture and labor, is considered quite average. They redecorate houses from top to bottom every time they move . . . and they move often. It's a rare Yank who's prepared to live with someone else's carpet or wallpaper. Not only does it cramp his style, but "you never know what they've done on it."

Ameri-home is the obvious physical expression of the American Dream. By Euro-standards, even your average shack is "super-equipped." It has Kleenex in every room. It has air conditioning, microwaves, media centers, computerized security systems, and automatic ice-cube dispensers. It has intercoms, piped-gas barbecues, water-and-air purifiers, sprinkler systems, and remote-controlled garage doors. Americans are probably the only people in the world who can't contemplate life without a built-in garbage compacter.

HOME AS CAMOUFLAGE

———————— B R I T - T H I N K ————————

There is beauty (and safety) in anonymity . . . which may explain why middle-class dwellings from one end of the country to the other are nearly identical. Brits in every income bracket short of the very top dislike domestic ostentation, and decline to call attention to their homes ("just so long as it's tidy"). They are happiest with formula floor plans and "traditional" features. From Washington New Town to Weybridge, proud owners peep from behind net curtains and leaded lights.

Round about the 1920s, a little-known architectural genius designed the first-ever bay-windowed semi-detached. A grateful nation has reproduced it ever since (with only minor modifications) from Cornwall to Aberdeen. It is etched on the nation's consciousness; felt to be the perfect dwelling, and the one which best suits and accommodates the British Way of Life. It is somehow "right." The only thing "righter" is a (period) house in the country, if you can afford one. But flats are not right—nor are open-plan rooms, double-volume spaces, warm-air central heating, soaring two-story windows or radical design statements. These are regarded as architectural perversions, which inevitably distort life within. Prince Charles is publicly scathing about new buildings that use too much glass.

Brit-homes have no equipment at all. Somewhere in the backs of Brit-minds, an indoor loo-with-low-flush-mechanism is still perceived as a "luxury" (the most overused word in the real estate agent's lexicon). The heating system doesn't work, though exposed radiators deface every wall surface and scald the cat. For reasons few can explain, Brits will spend many happy hours reading and talking in front of a false fireplace. (They are irresistibly drawn to any hint of neo-Georgian fiberboard surrounding an area of blank wall.) This is Spiritually Right, and reinforces traditional family values. Home is where the hearth isn't.

Brits haven't much need for interior designers, since the last thing they're after is showiness, idiosyncrasy, or display. (That's reserved for gardens and "grounds.") Only *two* decorative themes are allowable, and these are repeated the length and breadth of the nation:

1. *For the affluent, aspirational, or upwardly mobile:*
   The "country house" style. This calls for a great deal of antique furniture (reproductions if you can't afford the real thing), dark woods (mahogany is favored), gilded mirrors, floral fabrics and swagged velvets, well-worn Oriental rugs (nothing new, and *never* "washed Chinese") and subdued color schemes. Anything, in fact, which looks inherited and suggests Old Money. Can be scruffy, since Old Money often is.

2. *For everyone else:*
   Post–Second World War Ugly. Main design feature is carpets, fabrics, and wallpapers which jar horribly, and look as if they've ended up in the same room only because of "shortages." (Brit-style seems permanently circumscribed by the postwar period.) Favored color

schemes run to avocado-cream-brown, or alternatively black-with-orange blobs. Or both.

Time-honored Features and Principles of Brit-design:

1. *Never buy new furniture.*
Furniture is something you replace only when the old stuff wears out . . . never for aesthetic reasons. ("I know it's thirty years old, but it's a perfectly good couch.") When forced to buy new, choose something which looks old, thus reinforcing links with family and tradition. When you move to a new house, take old pieces with you—however out of place they seem in new surroundings. Sentiment should outweigh other considerations. It is un-British to redecorate from scratch.

2. *Find a focal point for your room.*
The false fireplace will do, or a three-barred radiant heater, or a coffee table. Whatever you decide, this *must* (for lo, it is written) be surrounded by three pieces of furniture: one sofa and two chairs.

3. *Welcome to my nightmare.*
Choose furnishing patterns purely because you *like* them, and not because they complement each other. Brown and black swirls in the carpet, pastel roses on the wallpaper, Art Deco zigzags in primary colors for the curtains. You know you've succeeded when you get carsick just sitting on the sofa.

4. *Create carpet interest.*
Whatever you do, avoid running one carpet choice throughout the house. The various patterns are specially effective where they join at doorways.

5. *The importance of lighting.*
Opt for the subtlety of a single bulb, hanging on an exposed wire from the center of the ceiling. For added interest, cover with fabric shade in bordello-red or cream. Control with hanging light cord. (Replace when grubby.) If forced to use wall light switches, place high enough so that they can just be reached on tiptoe.

6. *Accent with pictures . . .*
hung too high up the wall for anyone at ground level to see without spraining neck muscles. Then hang

decorative mirror high on opposite wall, perfectly placed
to reflect junction with ceiling.

7. *Every boudoir should have one.*
   There's a law somewhere in the Brit decorating canon
   which says that every bedroom must have a dressing
   table. This must have a mirror which must be placed at a
   bedroom window, so that the unpainted back is visible
   from the street.

8. *Hole idea.*
   Brit kitchens suffer from condensation. Remedy this by
   punching a hole in the kitchen window, with primitive
   cover operated by dirty string. Ventilator itself will also
   attract dirt, cause uncomfortable drafts, and breed a
   whole new strain of Legionnaire's Disease. It will do
   nothing, however, to alleviate the condensation—which is
   caused by time-honored Brit-building methods.

9. *No change.*
   Above all, your home must look and feel precisely like
   the one you grew up in. This is your chance to make
   time stand still. You may have an up-to-the-minute
   fashion sense, complete with magenta Mohican, but this
   will not extend to your surroundings, which Mummy will
   understand. Even leather-clad post-punk rockers still
   watch telly sitting on sage-green Dralon. All Brit-homes
   are clone homes.

SOME LIKE IT HOT

The greatest single difference between Brits and Yanks is in
common perceptions of heat and cold. It seems that natives of
each country possess internal thermometers—acquired at the
moment of birth—which remain unchanged even if they spend
many years abroad. Accents and attitudes may alter, but thermometers never do.

Americans are cold in Britain from the moment their planes
touch down at Heathrow. They're cold outdoors, and even
colder *in.* But they're coldest of all in the bathroom. There, their
suffering is complete . . . largely because of the British predilec-
tion for failing to heat toilet areas, then throwing windows open
in order to simulate latrine conditions.

Brits, while sympathetic at first, soon grow impatient with shivering Yanks, and advise them to wear more clothing. Americans pay scant attention. They hold the view that clothes are for aesthetic and fashion purposes only, and should not be required to do the job for which central heating was intended. They flatly refuse suggestions of thermal vests from Marks and Sparks. It's primitive to don extra layers when you can push up a thermostat. Anyway—after years of whole-grain diets and working out with weights, who needs to look fat? So, they continue to huddle miserably by heaters, and soon reach the conclusion that the refrigerator is the only thing in the average British home which is never cold.

THE HEAT IS ON

When in America, many Brits show sudden concern for the environment, and accuse Yanks of squandering energy resources. This is because they are very uncomfortable inside buildings, felled by the white-hot blast of serious central heating. They complain that it makes them dopey, and dries out nasal passages. (No one knows why they prefer wet ones.)

In America, Brits first experience *uniform* heating, having typically spent formative years searching for the warm spots in cold rooms. Suddenly, they are *parched.* They throw open hotel windows in a desperate bid to re-create drafts. Bowls of water placed by the bed simulate the general air of dampness they associate with home. Brits can't sleep in a room where there's no condensation on the mattress.

In fact, not only are they *grumpy* in wrap-around central heating . . . they are psychologically *distressed* by it. Heat, to be acceptable, must have a source—must be directional. For preference, it should come from the front (coal fires, gas or electric heaters), leaving your face flushed, your back and shoulders stiff and frozen. "Proper" heat is something around which a normal family can group the three statutory pieces of furniture. Try that around a warm-air duct.

•   •   •

ORDEAL BY WATER

It's a question of what turns you on, and what you turn on. Yanks believe that British bathrooms exist to mortify the flesh . . . (some people *like* it). Icy loo seats, abrasive toilet tissue, showers that don't work (inadequate water pressure) or spray everywhere (hard water sediment's bunged up the holes). If you're lucky, you get a thin trickle—useless for washing shampoo out of hair but perfect for flooding the floor. This is even easier when the shower curtain is missing. Brit bathrooms are not for sybarites. They are frosty places where one learns the true meaning of endurance. When the British army wants to go on survival training exercises, it spends two or three nights in a British bathroom.

Then there are Great British Bath Taps. Brits practice a kind of lavoratorial apartheid; hot-and-cold taps are separated as far as porcelain will allow, with nary a warm-water mixer in sight. One tap is scalding, the other is ice-cold. It tests initiative to regulate the flow to produce a mix of the required degree of warmness. By the time you discover your bath's too cold, you'll have exhausted the supply of hot water.

Some help is at hand in the form of the new, hi-tech British mixer. This produces not *warm* water, but parallel streams of hot and cold running from the same tap. There are myriad possibili-

ties for serious injury; and since spouts are placed as close to the sides of the basin as possible, it is virtually impossible to wet a toothbrush or fill a glass without risking collision.

BEDDY-BYE

Hardy Yanks who survive the rigors of a British bathroom and make it into bed are not home and dry. At least not *dry*. Apart from the dampness factor, there is the question of flatness. British beds aren't. The tops are stitched and tufted to make sure that:

1. you never enjoy a smooth night's sleep, and
2. lint of scientific interest gathers in the holes.

Traditional Brit-bedding is lumpy bedding. Furthermore, all-wool blankets of enormous hairiness are still preferred. They immobilize your legs under a great weight, and keep you in place —which is just as well, since Brit beds are very high, and if you roll out the fall can kill you.

SWEET DREAMS

An American's bed attests to his personal style in the same way as his home . . . and the more extravagant, the better. After all—it's a third of your life, and so on. Yanks sink their beds into carpeted platforms, hang them hammock-like on swinging chains, and install motors to make them tilt, revolve, and face the built-in media deck. Americans, too, have accidents while sleeping . . . but only if the waterbed bursts, causing short-circuits in the quadriphonic sound system and halogen light show.

CLOSET NEEDS

Americans like their closets to sleep four. All modern houses and apartments are supplied with spacious "walk-ins," which allow your clothes to live in greater luxury than some people. Chances are that you'll also have large mirrors—even three-way jobs—so that you can know the hideous truth about your rear end and trousers.

Brits have loads of clothing, but no closets. Old houses were built without them, and because "we've always done it this way," today's builders see no reason to change. Instead, they extol the virtues of "free-standing" wardrobes: "gives you such flexibility when planning your bedroom!" What it really offers is greater expense (you have to buy the wardrobes) and decreased floor space (the furniture takes up most of it).

Furthermore, Brit wardrobes are cunningly crafted to be a fraction less deep than the span of the average hanger when positioned on the rails. This means that the doors never close properly. The rail's so high that you can't reach it, and bows under the weight of even a few garments, allowing dresses and skirt hems to hit the floor. (Brit wardrobe manufacturers look harshly upon people with more than three changes of outfit.) And judging from the provision of mirrors, these should be viewed from the front only—and from the knees up.

5

CHOOSING PARTNERS...
"WHAT'S LOVE GOT
TO DO WITH IT?"

FIRST APPEARANCES

AMERI-THINK

"If I've only one life to live," breathes a beauty in a famous American TV commercial, "let me live it as a blonde!" As has been noted, it goes against the Ameri-grain to concede that "we pass this way but once." Just in case, however, true Yanks are determined to make the most of it. Appearance is vital. Suggest that beauty is only skin-deep, or that character counts most, and natural skepticism overwhelms them. It's all very well to have a fabulous personality; but—if you want to reach for the stars (and every American does)—you'll also need straight teeth.

They're equally pragmatic about nature and its wondrousness. "If nature's blown it, we'll fix it" is the national *cri de coeur* that's launched a million cosmetic operations. It's clear that the quality of your life—and your enjoyment of it—are largely dependent on the way you look. There's little doubt that appearance affects popularity, and financial success. "Just as God Made Me" is not always good enough. Look what He did with earwigs.

Ironically, Yanks—with most of life's basic necessities under wraps—are the world's greatest malcontents. They seek perfection, and cannot rest until they've made the best of a bad job. *Every* bad job. When it comes to themselves and their personal prospects, no effort is too great, no correction or refinement too insignificant, no orthodontist too expensive. Americans invest in themselves happily, guiltlessly. After all—when life is so precious, why waste a single day feeling bad about your nose?

This is the blessing and the curse of American affluence. If everything's possible, and no real obstructions stand in your way, you've no excuses. Failure is your fault. So is unhappiness.

─────────────── B R I T - T H I N K ───────────────

Nature usually gets it right the first time. Think carefully before pressing the override button. There's no such thing as perfection in this less-than-perfect world, and humans are no exception to the rule. What *is* success, anyway? How can you measure it, and what matter if you don't achieve it? Does British society respect you less if you're poor? (Yes.) Penalize you if you're stupid? (Of course.) Discriminate against you if you're unattractive? (Right on.)

To seek perfection is to commit the sin of hubris. Brits are fatalists . . . "we all die anyway." Why suffer and sacrifice for an uncertain (and inevitably temporary) gain? It is enough just to *be.* Avoid tampering, or trying too hard, which is unbecoming. Anyway—the class system gives you a natural place in the scheme of things. If you like, it's yours for life.

Yanks may believe that self-improvement = upward mobility = progress . . . but Brits hate the idea. For one thing, it suggests *change.* For another, it encourages a burst of personal initiative . . . your fate in your own hands, and so on. That idea makes Brits very tired. "Let It Be," sang Paul McCartney.

That goes for things physical as well. Why spend good money to straighten little Jeremy's peculiar teeth? Pure indulgence, when all mortals are flawed. If you're going to splurge, invest in something sensible—like a new stereo system.

MOUTHS

─────────────── B R I T - T H I N K ───────────────

Brits have some of the most curious dental configurations in the world. Their mouths often appear too small for a normal number of teeth. Anglo-orifices are tiny and discreet, nestling unobtrusively between nose and chin . . . (Mick Jagger's mouth is not orificially British). Brits keep stiff upper lips because they do not wish to call attention to their mouths by moving them. Large, wet, mobile apertures (like Mick's) strike them as obscene. Besides, they are hiding their teeth, since dental problems are woefully neglected. If there's one thing that frightens Brits more than the prospect of change, it's dentists.

—————————— A M E R I - T H I N K ——————————
Ameri-mouths are more generous, and usually open. This accounts for the difference between British and American *sandwiches*. Brits are forced to nibble thin cucumber ones because their mouths don't open wide enough to accommodate American whoppers. Ameri-jaws will separate at an angle of 180 degrees, no problem. Bring on the pastrami.

LET'S GET PHYSICAL: EVOLUTION OF THE YANK SPECIES

Physical perfection is supremely important in the selection of an Ameri-mate. First-class *appearance* is a reliable indicator of:

1. Intelligence. (You're smart enough to take care of your body.)
2. Self-esteem. (You like yourself well enough to want to.)
3. Affluence. (The peak condition of the thoroughbred can, to a large extent, be bought.)
4. Good genes. (Your biological inheritance.) Chances are that your progenitors were *also* all of the above. Ameri-masterpieces like you are no accident; they take generations to evolve.

In America, where there is no formal class-structure, fine physical appearance is a near-substitute. It's a mark of quality much sought after when Yanks wish to marry "up." In top American dynasties, family members seem to be uniformly smart, rich, and *beautiful.* Look at the Kennedys; a perfect example of selective breeding if ever there was one. Ditto Hollywood and "media" families. The litters produce few runts. Several generations of generous liquid assets, combined with heightened awareness of health and beauty (laced with public admiration), have produced beautiful parents producing beautiful children. And so Henry Fonda begat Jane, and Grace Kelly begat Princess Caroline, and Ernest Hemingway produced Margaux and Mariel, and Robert Mitchum several little Mitchums, and Edgar Bergen Candice, and so on. It seems to Americans that the very rich and famous are smart enough to be beautiful. What's luck got to do with it?

Mere mortals can only gasp, and imitate. This has led to a quest for physical perfection seldom seen since the days of Ancient Greece. Such is the popularity of health and beauty clubs that every new condo and place of work must have one. The national fixation with weight training, exercise, bran and stretch Lycra in assorted colors continues. Yuppies have deserted fashionable metropolitan singles bars and seek romance in private gyms. This is because:

1. Cocktails are high in calories and destroy both brain cells and Yuppie prospects.
2. The Mr. Right you meet at the rowing machine will have a high muscle-to-fat ratio, and a long life expectancy. Also, the price of membership to the gym.

Recognized signs to others that you are at the peak of physical condition, and therefore a desirable "catch," include:

1. Straight teeth. Also, *white* teeth. Any discoloration can be interpreted as nicotine stains.
2. Tight stomach muscles. When you are lying on your back, a wooden ruler should rest on both your hip bones without touching tummy. Flab is shmo.
3. A clear complexion (the outward sign of healthy eating), combined with well-conditioned hair that *moves . . .* (the forty-dollar cut).
4. Matching manicure. (See below.)

THE IMPORTANCE OF FINGERNAILS

Brits don't understand this. "Perfect down to the fingertips" is the main idea. All-American girls used to file theirs to graceful points, but no more. Experts on fingernail fitness decree that the sides are necessary for strength, and nail-structure improves if you square them off at the tops. Best physical specimens now have squared-off talons which attest to thirty-dollar manicures and sixty-dollar nail wraps.

Yankettes flash them a great deal when talking. They tap things for emphasis: table-tops, wineglasses, passages in newspapers, TV screens. They gesture extravagantly with their hands (why spend thirty dollars if no one notices?). They eat tons of gelatine for healthy nails (outward signs of a sound body), and when one breaks, it spoils the whole day. When they get engaged, their husbands-to-be (transfixed by their fingers) buy large diamond solitaires to set them off. These are cheap by comparison to the ongoing expense of nail care.

BRIT ENGAGEMENT RINGS

As comedienne Joan Rivers once said, staring incredulously at the third finger on a woman's left hand, "You *married* the guy who gave you that puny little ring?" Most Brits feel it's fine for tokens of affection to be *modest*. (NOTE: the Princess of Wales was not taken in by this one; when Charles offered his heart, she also collected a £50,000 sapphire.) Generally, Brits persist in the notion that love has nothing to do with money . . . that there's risk that the former will be vulgarized by the latter.

Eschewing ostentation as they do, even those with plenty of family money to spend will prefer:

1. Granny's inherited Victorian engagement ring
2. an antique engagement ring that *looks* like an inherited one
3. a new engagement ring of antique design

. . . to something modern and showy. If American taste runs to *rocks* like car headlights, Brit-bride chooses a discreet cluster of

---

mixed stones (traditionally diamonds with sapphires or rubies), each pin-prick gemette weighing in at .00001 carat, and nearly invisible to the naked eye. The ring is a maze of little platinum struts, topped with the merest hint of sparkle.

As a symbol, it's perfect. It's so clearly tasteful . . . like love. And personal. Like love. And sweet. Like love. And disappointing. Like love.

AMERI-ROCKS

Yankee brides *mistrust* small stones. The groom's investment in a ring is a deposit—an act of faith. It indicates that:

1. He cares. (He has adorned your body with something expensive.)
2. He intends to stay with you. (Your ring has absorbed all his money.)
3. He wants the best for you, so that:
4. He will work his socks off to make it all happen.

It's part of a marital pact; a question of mutual commitment and —perhaps more important—aspiration. A flashy ring is a symbol of your husband's intention to SUCCEED, and be a good provider. A puny ring is a symbol of his intention to stay a shlep.

6

THE IMPORTANCE OF
BEING "CUTE"

To succeed in America, you have to be "cute." This should be interpreted in its broadest sense, and is—in Ameri-minds—very nearly a metaphysical concept. It refers not just to endearing children (though it helps to start early if you want to get the hang of it). Cute also means arresting, appealing, charismatic, and satisfying. Spiritually, you are vibrating at the same frequency as Ameri-culture. This is the true meaning of success.

Anyone, anything, and any *idea* can be called cute—so the term is lavishly applied. Newborn babies are cute, Doppler radar is cute, Tom Selleck is cute, and so are Star Wars technology, raspberry popcorn, lots of sit-coms, and selected restaurants. Even serious corporations can get cute. An astute American businesswoman called Meg decided to name her financial consultancy "Meg-a-bucks."

"Cute" scratches a national itch. It describes everything you want someone (or something) to be. Cute is instant gratification, and wish-fulfillment. It has about it the delight of a fantasy-come-true. Presidents can be cute . . . virtually *have* to be video-cute in order to win. President Kennedy was very, very cute and he knew it. He was a national turn-on. Cute-looking, cute personality, and cuter sense of humor. Remember how cute he was when he arrived on his first presidential visit to France, and greeted cheering crowds with, "Hello. I'm the man who accompanied

Jackie Kennedy to Paris"? At times, it seemed he could do no wrong. Even Congress thought he was cute, which was important after the Bay of Pigs fiasco, which wasn't so cute. He was allowed to redeem himself with a successful conclusion to the Cuban missile crisis, which was pretty cute.

Many world leaders (including President Reagan but not Mrs. Thatcher) have drawn important lessons from this. President Reagan knows how to be cute (and little else). Nixon knew everything else, but wasn't a bit cute. Henry Kissinger could be cute-ish when he put his considerable mind to it. Caspar Weinberger is not one of life's natural cuties. The charm bred of gently self-mocking self-awareness—especially when deployed by public figures—is unstoppable. It works for the young, and for geriatrics. And if you're cute enough, you can have anything. America is up for grabs.

——————————— B R I T - T H I N K ———————————

The importance of being cute is only dimly perceived by Brits, with the possible exception of Robert Morley. Most British politicos, though, have miles to go before they can be considered fully humanoid, never mind seductive and appealing. Winston Churchill had bags of charisma, but was far too remote and intimidating a personality to be cute. Sir Harold Wilson has instinctive charm and the potential to be cute . . . but Mrs. Thatcher has *no* self-awareness, and cannot make her loyalest voters fall in love.

Of course, it is possible to be well-known and successful without being cute. But the latest scientifically designed "cuteness-factor" research shows that canny cuties surface faster—and get rich quicker. Here's the latest dipstick poll on Anglo-American cuteness:

· · ·

AMERI-CUTE:

Goldie Hawn is so cute you could throw up.

Ditto Liza Minnelli and Drew Barrymore.

Ronald Reagan is cute.

Nancy isn't.

Ron and Nancy together are perceived as "cute" by those Americans who like watching senior citizens hold hands.

There are people who think John McEnroe is cute.

There is no one who thinks Jimmy Connors is.

Bruce Springsteen does not like being considered "cute," but when you are worth a hundred zillion dollars, you live with it.

BRIT-CUTE:

The Queen and Prince Philip are far too grand to be "cute" together in public. This is because they are not required to win elections.

Mrs. Thatcher doesn't comprehend the importance of being cute.

Husband Dennis does, but Margaret cramps his style.

Boy George is too cute for his own good.

Dudley Moore is English and cute.

Michael Caine is Cockney and cute.

Rod Stewart is Scottish and cute, if you ask Britt Ekland. If you ask anyone else, he is Scottish.

Prince Charles is cute, ears notwithstanding. Could be even cuter if he'd let himself. If you are rich and Royal, it is nearly impossible not to be *devastatingly* cute . . . but because he is square, he has managed.

Brits often dismiss cuteness as intellectually crass. It is merely another form of Ameri-hype, to which finer minds are immune. Brit-feelings run deeper, and their spirits are far less easily galvanized (only by the Royal Family, Bob Geldof, First Division football clubs, or any mention of the Second World War). Yanks, on the other hand, can be aroused by almost anything.

An emotional bumper sticker. A pompom display by the Dallas Cowboys' cheerleaders.

Unless restrained, Americans take cuteness to saccharine extremes ("Shirley Temple syndrome"). Only they could tolerate the spectacle of Ron and Nancy walking hand-in-hand into a Republican sunset. Or invent Coca-Cola corporate ads. Or thrill to the beauty secrets of Linda Evans, or sit through syndicated reruns of *The Love Boat.*

COZYING-UP

But Brits shouldn't feel smug. They have their own version of surrender to popular myth, and it's called "coziness." As a state of mind, it's just as inert and self-congratulatory as cuteness. It is wholesale, blanket satisfaction with all things British . . . a kind of institutionalized self-love. Coziness is centrally generated by the BBC, which postulates a national attitude with every minute of airtime, daring people to depart from it. The Beeb is honor, goodness, and truth. The Beeb is family, the Civil Service, and the Queen. The Beeb is . . . Us. How cozy.

If cuteness fills Ameri-hearts with optimism, so does coziness arouse self-esteem in Brits. It promotes a sense of uniqueness, worth, and particular charm: "There are no others like us," "Brit is beautiful," "Nobody does it better." This conveniently reinforces the status quo, since coziness contains no suggestion of the need for change.

Loving the Royal Family is fundamentally cozy. The two-week observance of Brit-Christmas is cozy. Gardening is cozy, forming orderly queues at the slightest provocation is cozy (Brits pride themselves on waiting their turn in all things). Most news coverage is excruciatingly cozy, dwelling on the detritus of Brit-life at the expense of the larger, international story. Island-think.

All this contributes to an exceptionally cozy self-image. Brits see themselves as well-behaved people, honorable, fair-minded, and moderate. This in spite of years of class division, colonial rule, industrial strife, and football hooliganism. Cozy ideas are those which support this perception—especially at the expense of other "less well-behaved" nations.

7

SEX

Differences between Anglo- and Ameri-sex are mostly *oral*. Which is to say that Yanks talk more *about* it, then talk more while *doing* it, since sex in America is the stuff of endless self-examination. Brits are somewhat less introspective about sex, though the gap has been narrowing since the sixties. In general, they like to "get on with it," while Yanks experience full erotic catharsis only if they've talked it through first.

The main thing that British men will notice about American women is how much they talk. The average Yankette will probably utter 30 to 50 percent more words in a lifetime than her UK counterpart. It takes this much verbiage to tell people about herself ("lay herself entirely open") and to broadly explain her expectations (so that the "relationship" can begin on a sound footing, the possibilities of misunderstanding minimized).

Ms. Yank doesn't want a lot: merely to be blissfully happy, extravagantly rich, acclaimed for her achievements and personal style, idolized by her husband and children, publicly perceived as divinely beautiful, and on first-name terms with the President. And she wants her partner/husband to make it all happen (Having It All) while at the same time providing regular and euphoric sex.

— A M E R I - T H I N K —

Ameri-male knows where his duty lies. He's read the books and magazines which say she needs to feel independent and capable, yet needed and passionately desired. He's not stupid. It's been a long time since the sixties, when he painfully learned

new "responses" toward women, and purged traces of revision-
ist Male Chauvinist Pig thought. Now, he's a New Man; eyes
open, consciousness raised. We're talking *earnest* here. Yes, for
Yuppie Man (and influential Baby-Boomers) at least, years of
feminist agitation (words again) have at last begun to change
attitudes. What was hip affectation, mere lip service to women,
has gone deep throat. Payoff time. We've entered the First Age
of Post-Tokenist America.

This does *not* mean that women have finally caught up with
men in terms of money, power, and job opportunity. (It's often
presented as significant that women control one-third of all the
wealth in America . . . but most of them are widows.) What it
does mean—to the sharp observer—are small but significant
changes in male behavior.

Take any Yuppie dinner party. *Who* dominates the conversation over the cold vegetable paté with fresh-tomato-and-basil
sauce? No, *not* the Gary Hart look-alikes reviewing the day's
vicissitudes on Wall Street. They are strangely silent, solicitous,
and attentive while the *women* de-brief. They do not compete,
they listen hard, paying the undivided attention which Brit-
woman reserves, in similar circumstances, for Brit-man. In Post-
Tokenist America, women expect to *steer* the conversation . . .
not merely to punctuate it with occasional girlish giggles.

Every so often the New American Man will interject. Nothing
macho about sport or finance calculated to seize control and
exclude the female company. Instead, he opens with something
about urban interior design, or educational theory. He may ask
to see pictures of other guests' children (and he won't be gauche
enough to assume that only the *mother* carries them). Then he
may offer to show some of his own.

────────────── B R I T - T H I N K ──────────────
Brit-woman has (anti–sex discrimination laws notwithstanding)
scarcely made it to the Tokenist—let alone Post-Tokenist—Age.
Years of pro-feminist conditioning have not really cut across the
set of rigid social and sexual boundaries fixed in the minds of
Brit-males. In spite of herself (and her raised consciousness), Ms.

Brit spends a lot of time being grateful to men for small favors. She reacts this way to bosses, sons, and lovers. She shares her mother's conviction that you can get what you want without confrontation by applying a little "female psychology," and "humoring him." Let him think it's his idea.

In this way, Brit-woman dooms herself to a life of good-natured helplessness. She has no real power base, and lacks the courage to take the spotlight and stand her ground. She is apologetic about raising the subjects which interest her most, and—in mixed groups—covers them fleetingly, badly, assuming that she is boring the men present. She feels presumptuous when required to engage a husband's attention on a "feminine" issue . . . the choice of wallpaper, for example, or her approaching hysterectomy . . . thus dragging him from more pressing male concerns (the fortunes of Manchester United).

Progress at work is slow to nonexistent. Brit-male cannot bring himself to repose real confidence in her, and sees her rather as the monkey riding the bicycle. He does not expect her to do it well; the wonder is that she does it at all. Even when he likes her, and recognizes her abilities and achievements, he is unlikely to push for her promotion. (Brits like good things to stay *as they are.*) Furthermore, he cannot see her as a serious answer to corporate problems. If she shows any inclination to hustle, or force his hand —if, for one moment, she betrays her ambition—she will lose his goodwill. He will automatically obstruct her. He doesn't know why, but he can't help himself.

In Britain, only *women* have read the right magazines (or articles on "women's pages" in newspapers) since real men have better things to do with their time. Brit-woman is primed to expect a shift in attitudes, a new form of "sexual contract" along American lines . . . and she's prepared to keep her side of the bargain. (Problem is, she's the only one who *knows* there's a bargain.) So she's motivated to become a better and more interesting person, to dress well, diet, keep fit, and otherwise hold back the ravages of time. *He* does not always return the compliment, preferring to sit carpet-slippered in his favorite armchair and/or oldest jeans, eyes fixed firmly on the telly, fist clenching a can of something, teeth in desperate need of smokers' tooth polish. He is, he's convinced, a prize. "After all, I'm *here,* aren't I?" What he means is that she's lucky he's at home filling the armchair, when he could be out boring some other nice girl to death.

MARRIAGE OF TRUE MINDS

—————————— B R I T - C O U P L E S ——————————

The thing that strikes a Yank most forcibly on overhearing a conversation between a British husband and wife in a restaurant, or on a train, is that they carry on as if they've never met each other before. What, Yanks wonder, have they been *talking* about for the past twenty years?

The point is that Brits are great respecters of each other's privacy (which is another way of saying that they don't communicate much). They are careful not to "intrude," even in close family situations. This is evident in relationships between parents

and children, where grown-ups believe in "butting out" and letting little Oliver or Fiona make their own mistakes. Brit-parents are frequently seen to stand back while the sprogs head straight for the precipice, putting a brave face on things and cheerfully skating over the formalities of conversation.

──────── A M E R I - C O U P L E S ────────

Yanks, on the other hand, (because they talk so much) have long ago exhausted most conversational generalities and worked down to the gory details. They consider that intimacy confers a kind of emotional *carte blanche,* and use it without reservation to save their nearest and dearest from themselves. They worry away at their "relationships," examining, probing. Every psyche is up for grabs. Being in love means never having to back off.

So, there's lots of gratuitous comment on each other's "hang-ups" and "real motivations." Americans are the world's greatest psycho-nags. Cruel—and amateur—dissections are commonplace.

BRITS AND YANKS IN LOVE

Brit-male resists falling in love in the first place by adopting an attitude toward women which is . . . dismissive. He often casts them as "joke" figures, which relieves him of any need to treat them seriously. The precise way in which this is done varies from region to region, but a short acquaintance with TV comedy reveals that:

1. In the South
   She is often portrayed as brainless and oversexed. After he nails her, he can't remember her name. Nor she his.
2. In the North
   Sex is, for him, a purely passive affair, in which she is the voracious predator. He runs for his life from her unsolicited attentions, much preferring a game of snooker with the lads. For her part, when she is not

running salivating after him, she is bending iron bars
with her bare hands.

What with one thing and another, it is easy to form the impression that Brit-male does not really like women much. This is not
true. He does, in fact, desire them passionately, and is inclined
to pursue them, as long as he does not have to talk to them too.

American women generally find British men attractive and
sexy, and are often prepared to marry them—i.e., Linda and Paul
McCartney, Chris Evert and John Lloyd, Wallis Simpson and
King Edward VIII, Caroline and Tony Wedgwood Benn, and
Winston Churchill's mum and dad. With rare exceptions, this is
a mistake, since America is something of a matriarchy, while
Britain (Mrs. Thatcher notwithstanding) is not. If Yankette simply does what comes naturally, every lovers' tiff will bring with
it the charge that she is "pushy" and "aggressive" . . . or just
plain loud.

Of course, there are romantic compensations. He "speaks so
beautifully" (when he speaks). An English accent sounds far
more seductive than the casual Yank approach: "Hiya, kid,
wanna dance?" He uses expressions she's never heard on the lips
of a man, like "Oh, lovely" . . . causing her to wonder if he is
sensitive and passionate, or just gay. (Real Ameri-men don't eat
quiche or say "Oh, lovely.")

His relative diffidence presents problems, a lack of willingness
on his part to join her in analyzing the relationship. This comes
as something of a shock. Ameri-bride knows Brits to be an articu-
late people, skilled at public debate. But they seem to reserve
their best stuff for perfect strangers, or formal speaking engage-
ments, or the West End stage, or the floor of the House of
Commons, or the telly. They don't waste much energy at home.
After the first flush of a new relationship, love talk dries. Brits
quickly run out of steam and enthusiasm for examination and
appraisal. (No conversational staying power.) In fact, once married, they see no further *need* for conversation. This is why it
takes them ten to fifteen years to find out how their partners like
coffee.

SERIOUS SEX

Yanks Treat Sex Seriously (as they do all other areas of personal development). They approach it with the earnestness and single-minded determination you'd expect from a marathon runner in training. They mean to win, to experience the Ultimate Orgasm. And they like to do things scientifically.

God helps those who help themselves. As a college undergrad, Ameri-male has read all the right books, can reel off eighty-two erotic pressure points, thirty "most successful" positions, sixteen surefire manual techniques, and the location of the "G-spot." Like all Americans, he reposes great confidence in "expertise" (anything which is written down) and is concerned to achieve his own—and his partner's—full erotic potential. He is not a great lover, but he is *committed*. Someday, it may all come naturally, but not yet. He doesn't trust his own instincts, and it's a bit . . . deliberate. All his foreplay comes from page 25 of the *Superstud's Handbook*.

————————— B R I T - I N - B E D —————————

Nothing so testing for Super-Brit, who wouldn't dream of brushing up on technique, "something you're born with, or forget it." He prides himself on being instinctive in bed, which is not necessarily the same as "generous." To be fair, it is between the sheets that he seems to shine, to magically shed the plethora of inhibitions which dog the rest of his waking life. He becomes rather creative, certainly catholic in his tastes, and even *experimental*. A Brit experimental is a Brit abandoned.

POST-COITALLY...

Ameri-man will remain physically close to his partner, because it says in the book how much she hates it when men roll away and snore. Drained and exhausted, he turns mentally to page 26, and continues to demonstrate tenderness.

Super-Brit has no such reservations, reverting instantly to type . . . and usually to silence. If he knows the line, he muffs it. Instead of "I love you and I enjoyed it," he mutters something about enjoying you and loving it.

8

THE CHILDREN . . . BABY-BRIT, BABY-YANK

The whole purpose of Having It All is passing It All on to your children. No matter how humble your own origins, It All is your child's birthright. Remember that America is the Land of Opportunity where any kid can grow up to be President, even if her name is Lisa.

Today's Ameri-parents feel compelled to help a child get the jump on others. Gone are the days when you could sit back and let him develop at his own pace. The 1980s are all about the survival of the fittest; and a parent's highest duty is to position pride-and-joy for success. Ameri-kids in the fast track need to progress:

1. from neonatal sensory training, to
2. the best Montessori preschool, to
3. early kindergarten entrance, and
4. the city's top-rated elementary school with "advanced ability" classes or a "gifted" program, to
5. the most competitive junior high and high school, with the vital run-up to S.A.T.s and possible early admission to
6. an Ivy League university with a first-rate reputation in pre-law, plus a grueling one-year cram-course to prepare for crucial L.S.A.T.s and
7. America's finest law schools, where a respectable performance leads at last to

8. partnership in a prestige law firm charging wildly exorbitant fees, and guaranteeing for progeny and progenitors

. . . a piece of the AMERICAN DREAM.

The fiercer the competition, the more determined is Ameri-parent. He will not let himself off the hook. If all things are possible, there is no reason for failure, apart from poor planning. At each step along the way his task is to help his infant jockey for a front position in the fray.

Can you call yourself a parent when your kid never: studied Suzuki violin/swam before he walked/read before he swam? Can you walk tall if he's not computer-literate at eight? Who's his private baseball/gymnastics coach? Is he enrolled at summer tennis camp? Has he seen a nutritionist/does anyone speak to him in Spanish/when does he get hidden braces on his teeth?

Yank parents seldom hold with the sentimental notion of loving and accepting a child simply for what he is. They love him, all right, but they're happy to try to improve upon nature. If he needs help, he gets help. His destiny is in their hands.

So, they set themselves the rather schizoid task of boosting the child's self-esteem ("Eric, you are a wonderful and worthwhile person . . . a winner!") while at the same time remaining detached enough to take an objective view. If Eric is stuck with a big nose, crooked teeth, a dud personality, and trouble with long division, all-American parents will fix it. They are the only parents in the world with the inclination and the resources to reassemble their kids if they don't like them.

No effort is too great. Enormous amounts of time, energy, and money are expended on Ameri-kid in the fond hope that, someday, even the least promising specimen will turn up trumps. He'll be a credit to his parents; President, perhaps, or better still—rich. Interestingly, however much time he spends being hot-housed to perfection, he spends still more engaged in one vital and patriotic activity: GOING OUT TO DINNER. Yes, Ameri-parents take their children everywhere, since junior is entitled to the best, and "the best" is defined by what his parents do. They like to "expose" him to everything (diseases apart). He is the focus of all their attention, and they are inordinately proud of him . . . even if he's at a relatively primitive stage of development. They're constantly torn between conflicting desires to compliment him and nag him to death. They compromise by doing both, and taking an obsessive interest in every fiber of his (by now ample) being. Ameri-parents characteristically probe the infant psyche as they do each other's in romance, examining, analyzing, discussing. He has no place to hide. He is their Great White Hope, and they reserve the right to drive him crazy while worshipping at the shrine.

——————— B R I T - T H I N K ———————

Brit-parents take a child more or less as he comes. If he comes with crooked teeth, they'll stay crooked. A weak chin will continue to recede. Not for them a survey of plastic surgeons, gathering opinions on whether to pin back his ears. Unless there's a medical imperative, Brits (including affluent ones) dislike interfering with nature. They will refine his natural attributes in two areas only:

1. His accent. This will concern them, as it must be *at least* as good as theirs, and if possible, better. If he fails to pass muster in this important respect, he is socially doomed . . . separated from his parents by the Brit-system of aural segregation. Stressful years are spent trying to counteract the influence of his scruffy friends, who can't complete a full sentence without a glottal stop . . . "'ullo, Mrs., c'n oi 'ave a bo'ull of soda?"
2. His table manners. These can truly affect his life. At the first opportunity his tiny fist is unclenched from the fork he wields like an ice pick. His earliest words are "Please-may-I-get-down?" By the time he is eight, he's taught to understand the proper use of a fish knife. If his

table manners are impeccable, the logic goes, no one will notice his teeth.

Brit-parent is, like his American counterpart, enormously proud of his offspring. But, for reasons he can't explain, he'd rather die than express it. There's a lot of good-natured banter about how hopeless little Jeremy is, usually conducted outside the child's earshot, with adult friends who can be counted upon to be just as disparaging about their own kids. This is a Brit-ritual which should not be taken at face value. Parents merely *pretend* to be detached, resigned, and objective so that real feelings are disguised; it's bad form to score points off another child, or to show off. In truth, they think that small Jeremy is bloody marvelous. Big ears and all.

The disparagement will continue—to a lesser extent—in front of the child him/herself. Not for Brit-kid the continually massaged ego of his American counterpart. Too much praise is not *good* for him. It will make him pigheaded and insufferable. Worse still, it may make him *precocious* (despised in a Brit-child, but much valued by American parents, who feel it's important to be *forward*). Brit-parents still consider that modesty and humility are virtues. Americans see them as self-imposed handicaps.

SPENDING TIME WITH THE KIDS

Ameri-parents are so publicly proud of their children (even while they're still at the awkward, prototype stage) that they

1. want to be near them all the time (i.e., in restaurants),
2. talk about them at the slightest encouragement (so certain are they that the finished product will be a knockout), and
3. assume that everyone else is smitten, and would like to spend time with them, too.

So, a word of warning: If British adults meet Americans on holiday (when it can be seen or assumed that the Yanks have brought young Eric along) Brits should be wary of making dinner arrangements unless they crave his company as well. Yanks openly admire their children, and wish to share them. They assume that you—a friend—will actually *want* to meet their relatives/kids/families . . . whereas Brits make the reasonable assumption that nothing could be further from your thoughts.

Brit parents do not by habit call attention to their children until they are young adults, and relatively presentable (capable of using a fish knife with confidence). The affluent upper (and upper middle) classes have for years operated a system of infant apartheid, under which children are treated as separate and unequal. In prosperous families they are kept under wraps for years, relegated to nannies and boarding schools. Years ago, Victorian parents did not formally meet their children until they'd reached seventeen.

The legacy of this system remains in many households. Children from up-scale families seldom eat an evening meal with their parents; at 5 P.M. or so, they take nursery tea with nanny. This is a traditional collation of stodge-on-starch (bread and butter with biscuits and cakes) devised in days when no one understood the connection between protein and growth. The practice survives because this is Britain, and "We've always done it this way." Anyway, Brit-parents seem to consider that children are only small, and do not need to eat like real people.

Such children also wear short pants in December, because "They don't feel the cold." No one knows if they experience pain. This is why Brits maintain corporal punishment in schools, and feel there is an argument for walloping people too little to fight back. (Brits pride themselves on being a civilized lot, and are one of the only nations in the world too humane to beat convicted criminals. They do it to their children instead.)

They also scrimp and sacrifice to send them to boarding schools of Draconian comfortlessness, which they attended themselves and which ruined their own childhoods. They do this because "One does," and because it "develops character" (not to mention head lice). Most important, it Teaches One How to Behave. In short, it encourages impressionable kiddie-clone to imitate the mannerisms of everyone else at boarding school, so that he can for evermore recognize and be recognized by members of his own social set. He is now equipped with *British Radar.* Entrée into his exclusive club is the Anglo version of designer labeling.

WHAT'S IN A NICKNAME?

Brits take names Very Seriously. They treat their own with great respect (since they are part of proud traditions of class and family) and resist shortening them. Yanks—who can rarely trace their ancestors or their names back further than Ellis Island—are more casual. Anyway—how protective can you be about Yablonsky or Lipschitz?

Everyone knows that Americans use names in conversation far more than the British do. When a Yank is introduced to you for the first time, he'll have a contest with himself to see how many times he can repeat your handle in a sentence. Names appeal to an American's sense of the importance of the individual . . . and he prefers first names to last ones. Using yours a lot is his way of getting friendly. He means it as a compliment—and each usage is testimony to your uniqueness as a human being. In Ameri-culture, overuse of a first name indicates that someone is paying attention to you. If it sounds ingratiating, it is also flattering.

Brits avoid using names if at all possible. To address relative strangers so directly strikes them as presumptuous . . . something of a liberty. They prefer to preserve a bit of distance. So, the higher your social status, the lower the likelihood of being called by name. Other Brits—as a courtesy and mark of respect—will simply pretend that you don't have one. Instead, they'll substitute official titles ("Hello, Chairman," or "Yes, Minister") or fall back on the anonymous "Certainly, Madame." Unlike Yanks, they will avoid referring to anyone as "Sir" unless he is a Peer of the Realm. Americans throw the term around, since it's no indication of rank. They call *everyone* "Sir" if they:

1. want to sell him something, or
2. mean to be nice, and
3. didn't catch his first name.

Furthermore, Americans like and cultivate nicknames, even when they are grown men at the top of the corporate or political tree. They do not feel demeaned by diminutives, or "cute" handles. (See "Cute," p. 41.) How else do you explain "Ronnie" Reagan, or "Jimmy" Carter, "Tip" O'Neill, "Bebe" Rebozo, or "Swifty" Lazar?

The truth is that nicknames make Americans feel *liked*—especially if they have an *ee* sound on the end: Judy, Janie, Dickie, Billy, Katie, Dougie, Wendy, Normie. Given the chance, they will tack an *ee* onto the unlikeliest names; if an English friend is called Nigel, he becomes "Nigey." If the proper name *already* contains an *ee* sound (i.e., Sidney) Yanks will rearrange it, so that it ends in an even more affectionate *ee*. For example, "Sidley." If you don't acquire an *ee* on the end of your name soon after Americans meet you, chances are that they don't like you much.

Yanks also enjoy choosing fairly brutal and insulting nicknames for male friends . . . particularly if these are shortened versions of unpronounceable Middle European surnames. Slobovoditch goes through life as "slob," Yablonsky as "yob," Buitoni as "boo-boo," and Spitalney as "spit." These are carried with pride, and often endure well into adult life.

The Brit version is a somewhat gentler affair, and usually a play on the last name, since parents are at pains to give first names which "can't be shortened." Every time they speak to little Nigel, or Olympia, or Tarquin, or call them to tea, they repeat the whole impressive handle. No Nige, or Ollie, or Tark. Mini-

Brits are encouraged to take themselves rather seriously in this respect.

As soon as they leave the house, the whole thing is up for grabs. Super-Brit surnames are specially at risk, and quickly reduced. "Faversham" becomes "Favvers," "Bothrington" equals "Bothers." If you're at boarding school, and unfortunate enough to be part of a family of boys called "Ramsbottom," it's Bottoms maximus and minimus. In the best circles, America's favorite ethnic nicknames are right out. It's safe to say that virtually no one at Eton or Gordonstown gets called "Bubulah."

Finally: it is a scientifically documentable fact that the *shorter* an adult male Brit is, the less likely he is to let you abbreviate his name. Forcing you to repeat eighteen syllables seems to increase his sense of stature. Just try calling Jonathan Frederick Hethrington-Spiers "Johnnie"—or "Jon Jon"—and see how he likes it.

. . .

WHAT'S IN A NAME

Yanks are never, ever called:
Nigel, Neville, Arabella, Tarquin, Sian, Fionna, Pippa, Dermot, Derek, Trevor, Gemma, Giles, Morag, Clyde, Coriander, Olympia, Nichola, Briony, Sebastian, Bronwyn, Candida, Philippa, Lavinia, Miranda, Tristram

Brits are never, ever called:
Murray, Seymour, Irv, Mitzi, Farrah, Ashley, Herb, Sheldon, Cuthbert, Billie-Jo, Adelaide, Ralph, Merv, Mindy, Candy, Sissy, Brooke, Shannon, Babe, Marcy, Melissa, Dwight, Duane, Buddy, Rock, Ridge, Tab.

In America, these are girls' names:
Robin, Jamie, Adrienne, Laurie, Leslie

In Britain, these are boys' names:
Robin, Jamie, Adrian, Laurie, Leslie

The American Nickname You Can't Have in Britian: RANDY. To Brits, it does not sound like a diminutive of Randolph. It is a bit like going around calling yourself "sex-crazed."

9

ASPIRATIONS . . . OR "YOU CAN'T HAVE EVERYTHING—WHERE WOULD YOU PUT IT?"

HAVING IT ALL

A M E R I - T H I N K

Life is about Having It All—the most American of catch phrases. This has replaced the discredited idea that "you can't have everything," which now sounds quaint and old-fashioned. Postwar Baby-Boomers—possibly the most influential members of Yank society—are convinced that you not only *can,* but *should*, have it all: beauty, intelligence, health, talent, money—and fame as a result. The catch is that nothing happens unless you *make* it happen. Hence, the compulsion to exercise, diet, wheel-and-deal, write books, appear on talk shows, and marry "up." Also to live forever, since there's scant time for total success in one lifetime. Even TV commercials appeal to the Yank's sense of comprehensive ambition; the slogan for Michelob Lite beer runs, "Oh, Yes, You *Can* Have It All!"

Recent changes in television shows document the shift in attitudes. Three of today's brand leaders are *Dallas, Dynasty,* and *Falcon Crest*—serials depicting the world of the super-rich. Their popularity suggests that the American Dream has been upgraded . . . from the sweet, suburban comforts depicted in *Father Knows*

Best, Ozzie and Harriet, and *The Life of Riley,* to hard-core mega-wealth and all its privileges—including the freedom to be nasty. The Carringtons are fascinating because they let Americans see why and how the rich are different.

New American role models are those who fend for themselves (Rambo) and get their own way. "Go for it!" is the buzz word. People who've taken the idea to heart include athletes, rock stars, models, businessmen, newscasters, and even TV weathermen. Many enjoy huge incomes, and convince themselves that "I deserve it." The syndicated television series *Lifestyles of the Rich and Famous* illustrates the material rewards of Me-think, and is a runaway success. The problem is that the possibility of Having It All is a mixed blessing. Many Americans are now restless . . . confused about how best to invest their energies. The question on nearly 250 million pairs of lips is, "If it's all within reach, if I can have it all—why haven't I *got* it? How can I get it? And when is enough enough?"

MUDDLING THROUGH

B R I T - T H I N K

Brits feel no desire to Have It All. They were so relieved to learn that "you can't have everything." They prefer to relax, and enjoy working within life's natural boundaries—"I'm not very good at games"—instead of kicking against them. As a nation, they are so fond of limitation that where necessary, they will invent one: "You're not the type to wear red"; "He's not well suited to business."

Brits hate being required to hustle and change the course of destiny—even in their own interests. They have a great and easy capacity for contentment, and can derive much satisfaction from small successes: "Look, dear, I've cleaned the fish pond." It's not —as is often said—that they are lazy. But they've seen the future, and decided that it doesn't work, and is not worth getting hot and bothered about. They are united in the belief that most change is neither possible nor desirable . . . which also rules out improvement. So, Brits of all classes live for the moment. They have no master plan, no ultimate ambition: "What's it all about, Alfie?" As a group, they are a bit chaotic. It is a particularly British concept to "muddle through."

This distinguishes them from Yanks, who are in every sense goal-oriented . . . "I always do twenty-seven laps before breakfast"/"I want to be a millionaire before I'm forty." In general, Brits are less single-minded and determined. Their private aspirations—if they can be identified, since they embarrass Brits—are more modest: "This year, Muriel, I'll wipe out the greenfly."

Historically, Brits have been wary of men of driving ambition. ("That's how you get dictators. Or trade-union bosses.) It's a romantic notion, anyway, for any one of us to think we can change the world. Silly to believe there's a reason why our own interests should prevail. That way lies ruin . . . look at the Second World War. Far better to relax, and cultivate your own garden. Anything for a quiet life.

Yanks want to know why we're here. They're desperate to leave a mark on life, to impose some order on the chaos. They need to decide if it's all about money, or power, or love, and act accordingly. Brits *know* why we're here. In the words of the song, "We're here because we're here."

BRIT-SOAP

If the formula for American soap opera is high life and success, Brits prefer low life and failure. As Yanks sit transfixed by the private lives of oil tycoons, Brits dwell on the meager surroundings of the socially deprived. Hence, the continuing popularity of *Coronation Street* and *East Enders.* If the glossy images and fantasies peddled on *Dallas* and *Dynasty* are gratifying to one side, long-running sagas of grinding poverty are just as compelling to the other. Brits seem to find them soothing. They provide proof—if any is needed—that most men lead lives of quiet desperation: nasty, brutish, and short. They match the national pessimism about

1. things changing for the better.
2. things changing at all.

Yanks find it thrilling to think there are yet more dizzying heights to achieve; Brits find it comforting to know that there's always someone worse off than *you* are.

STRIKE IT RICH

AMERI-THINK

It follows that Americans generally want to, while Brits aren't that bothered. A favorite T-shirt, often seen on the streets of Manhattan, encapsulates Yank-think. It reads, "Whoever Has the Most Things When He Dies Wins." In the absence of other criteria for success, goods and assets will do. Life is very nearly quantifiable in cash terms. For instance: Yanks have never really believed that "money won't buy health." No one who's had dealings with the American medical profession would swallow that. As smart old Sophie Tucker once said: "I've been rich . . . and I've been poor. And rich is better."

BRIT-THINK

In 1985, when the pound was in crisis and sliding disastrously against the dollar, President Reagan said of the British: "I think they have a way to go in changing some rigidities in their customs and methods of doing business." This endeared him to few, and made it clear that his ignorance of Brit-think is complete. Little does he know that Brits cherish the "rigidities" in the system, and seek to preserve them . . . that they do *not* sincerely want to be rich. (Well, not that much, anyway. Wouldn't say no to a win on the pools.) Such an idea is entirely outside his experience, and as outlandish as suddenly being told that Nancy has an obesity problem.

No: Britain is not a failed version of the U.S. financial model. It fails on its *own* terms. The structure is a dead weight, bearing down equally on the "Them" side and the "Us" side, ensuring paralysis and a certain symmetry. To Yank amazement, the British public seems content, and will vote in huge numbers for any party promising not to change a thing.

. . .

SUCCESS STORY

Generally, Brits feel that to succeed—especially in financial terms—is, proportionately, to deprive someone else. They see society's resources as finite, so too great a concentration in individual hands is greedy and antisocial. This perception is not exclusive to socialists, but is often shared by those on the political right: "We-think." Achievement must be tempered with a sense of social responsibility. Brits don't like piggies, and will unite in condemnation of anyone suspected of trying to corner a market.

Brit-censure does *not* extend to high-profile figures awash with *inherited* wealth. Even the poorest of the poor feel no resentment toward the Queen or Royal Family, with their vast (tax-free) incomes and estates. This is because it's not the Queen's *fault* that she is rich. God knows, she didn't try, and it's probably a worry to he   ̄ʋneasy lies the head that controls the Crown Estates.)

ʋlf-made men are admi   ʋʕSir Freddie Laker, Sir Clive Sinclair) as long as they don't push   ʋs too far (*folie de grandeur*). Brits are pessimists, believing that many   ʋʕ for the stars ends in a fall to earth. They often warm more to   ʋn the way down (Sir Freddie Laker). Ideally, achievement should appear effortless. Success—unless it's somewhat fortuitous—can look grubby and gauche. Failure is at the very least decorous, and rather dignified. *Cosier* than unmitigated success.

Nothing succeeds like success/Having It All/You've come a long way, baby/You're only as good as your last picture/All that counts is the bottom line. Success is literal, tangible. It usually brings material rewards. You can't be successful in a vacuum since success must be apparent, and recognized by all. There are exceptions ("I'm a good mother")—though, to be frank, Americans find self-proclaimed success less convincing.

Yanks have no problem with the ambitious, or financially acquisitive. Society's resources (like its opportunities) are infinite; therefore, you can climb to the highest heights without appreciably harming me. There's plenty for everyone, more for smart guys. Moral: Be a smart guy.

Americans favor a pragmatic approach to success. Do what you have to do as long as

1. it's legal, and
2. it works.

When it *stops* working, get out quick with a blanket over your head. Yanks have little patience with failure.

FAILURE: ANGLO-AMERICAN EXCUSES

MAKING DRAMAS OUT OF CRISES

BRIT-THINK

Since no one expects things to work, Brits are very tolerant of explanations for why they haven't. "It can't be helped," they shrug, resigned. Brits like things that can't be helped. The weather, for example. Or train derailments. Or power failures, or national strikes. They are very fond of acts of God—or indeed any situation which allows them to "soldier on," vowing to "muddle through somehow." Brits get Brownie points for "making the best of a bad job." (This of course relieves you of any obligation to do a *good* one.)

Brits are adept at making the most of even minor setbacks. Because they have so few natural catastrophes on a grand scale (earthquakes, typhoons, volcanoes, blizzards), they've learned to make full use of the ones they've got. The whole nation grinds to a halt because of delays in first-class postal service. Or dead leaves on railway tracks.

When business fails to profit, Brits are glad to accept "acts of God" explanations. The problem is not poor planning, or woeful decisions; it's the unexpected rise in interest rates/devaluation of the yen/monsoons in Sri Lanka/collapse in oil prices. Less is mentioned about inaccurate research, failure to predict trends or contain damage. It's "victim syndrome"—otherwise known as BRITVIC. Ask a Brit what he wants to be when he grows up, and the honest answer is "a victim of circumstances."

DELEGATING BLAME:
"IT'S 'A NOTTA MY FAULT!"

A U.K. press report on the Queen's visit to California commented on the ugliness and inappropriateness of one beribboned evening dress in the official wardrobe. "In choosing it," the journalist concluded, "the Queen was badly advised." "IT'S 'A NOTTA HER FAULT!" She was but a passive victim, unable to influence events. Never let it be said that Her Majesty made an error of judgment. Off with a minion's head.

Brits are masters at delegating blame, which is why "advisers" are so handy. Royal families seem to have zillions. In all walks of life "professional advice" is highly regarded, and generally deferred to. In this way individuals are separated from the responsibility for their own decisions. "Counsel" tells you whether or not to bring a court case, and you seldom seek a second opinion. Nor do you question "professional" judgment: "the doctor booked me in for an operation/teacher says Trevor's not university material/my bank manager told me I'd be able to afford the payments." There's no need to do something difficult —like think. Your fate is in someone else's hands. That way, there's always someone to behead when things go wrong.

——————— A M E R I - T H I N K ———————
Americans only *pretend* to delegate. Anything. As Harry S. Truman once said, "The buck stops here." They suffer from a pathological fear of "losing control," and a paranoid suspicion that, given a half a chance, others will "screw you up." Or at least treat your interests more casually than they would their own.

They're happiest keeping a firm grip on events, and asking a lot of questions. It's the boss's job to choose the right advisers, and his fault if they goof. (This is occasionally true in Britain as well, but only in the case of politicians—where a Ministerial *faux pas* can bring down the Government—or in football, when the team loses games and the manager gets sacked.)

Yanks adore results, and have scant interest in the rationale for failure. They do not consider it ruthless to discard something—or someone—that hasn't worked. There's little sympathy for "bad luck" or even "acts of God." Furthermore, Yanks do not believe in "accident." There is simply no such thing, and here they are hard-boiled. "You should've seen it coming. You should've been better prepared." The Reagan administration took enormous flack for failing to anticipate the suicide bomb attacks on U.S. Marines in Beirut.

Fault is always attributable. Occasionally, there are such things as extenuating circumstances ("I fired in self-defense"), but, in general, mainstream Yank-think sees most excuses as lame ones. "I was knocked unconscious at the crucial time." No good. You should've been more alert, or in better physical shape. Yanks associate failure with malingering . . . or crass stupidity. Either way, they don't like being taken for a ride. And they don't like paying for what they don't get.

What they deeply love is *success.* The very word sends shivers up Yank spines. Pragmatists all, they admire things which work, and adore the party responsible. Make a good business decision, or a wise choice of girlfriend/boyfriend, and you'll enjoy unqualified approval. After all, there's no such thing as "accident." If you've merely been lucky, you'll nevertheless be declared "smart."

How do you know when you've succeeded? You know when someone else tells you. *Anyone* else. In general, Yanks lack confidence in their own tastes and decisions, and long for feedback from others. They feel safest when all choices are officially "approved" (hence the popularity of Gucci belts, initial scarves, Nike sports shoes, Burberry raincoats, and designer jeans). It follows that a good decision is one that's *endorsed.* Success seems "real" only if it is reflected in the eyes of another. Even if he's a real shmo.

·   ·   ·

BOUNCING BACK

BRIT-THINK

Brits don't recover from adversity. The perpetuation of problems is a point of some national pride. Never quit when you're on a losing roll. Heroism is about the struggle against adversity . . . the triumph over it merely a footnote. Take the Second World War. Nice to win it, of course; but the most gratifying part was the bit about holding out with courage and dignity.

In fact, so uncomfortable are Brits with real victory that they have spent the past forty years trying to redress the balance. Thanks to their unstinting efforts, the prime movers on the losing side now enjoy far healthier economies than Britain's.

SETBACKS

It is good form—and a mark of attractive humility—to be properly set back by setbacks. Small ones will do. This is not a nation of bouncers-back; all obstacles are regarded as major, all defeats as permanent. So people will entertain, as serious propositions, any of the following: "He was never the same after his plumbing business collapsed." "Her life was ruined when she had to go to court on that parking charge, and then her daughter got divorced." "It finished her off when the corner laundrette closed down."

In short, Yanks accept few excuses for failure, but see no reason why you can't begin anew. As often as necessary. There *is* life after defeat. Brits accept many reasons for failure, but seem determined to go down with their ships. This is because they do not fully believe in the possibility of fresh starts. Something in the national temperament makes them reject alternatives, and forgo second chances. The captain of the *Titanic* stood stoically on the bridge as she sank, murmuring, "Be British!"

10

THE FOOD
CONNECTION

Brits have a problem with pure pleasure. They feel guilty about wallowing in food like continental types; one should eat to live, and not the other way around. The traditional British diet reflects this sense of gastronomic utilitarianism. It runs to cold pork pie, sausages, offal (heart, tripe, braised kidney), zillions of things on toast (meat paste/cheese/baked beans/spaghetti) and zillions of permutations on the general theme of mince (i.e., shepherd's pie). The best thing that can be said for this sort of Brit-fare is that, in the short term, it keeps you alive. In the long term, it probably kills you.

Though Brits are slowly becoming more diet-and-health conscious (bearing in mind their natural resistance to change), many food favorites bear more relation to solid fuel than nutrition as we know it. It must be remembered that middle-aged Brits grew up in the postwar years, with their legacy of basic food shortages and ration books. An egg was a luxury, many fruits and vegetables scarce. But there were heavy syrup puddings, and cakes made with lard. Mum needed two strong men and a forklift truck to remove baked goods from the oven.

·   ·   ·

EATING IN BRITAIN: THINGS THAT CONFUSE
AMERICAN TOURISTS

1. Why do Brits like snacks that combine *two starches?*
   (a) If you've got spaghetti, do you really need the
   toast?
   (b) What's a "chip-butty"? Is it fatal?
2. Why is British pie crust removed from the oven
   while the dough is still raw and white?
3. Is bread-with-dripping a form of mass suicide which
   involves voluntarily clogging your own arteries?
4. Is cockaleekie the curse of the permissive society?
5. What is Marmite? What are Ribena and Lucozade?
   What is their connection with the British Way of Life
   and the War Effort?
6. Why are they nuts about Weetabix . . . the only
   breakfast cereal designed to disintegrate into mush on
   first contact with milk?
7. Why do they call cake "gateau"? Why is the icing on
   a birthday gateau hard and thick enough to prevent
   nuclear meltdown?
8. Sandwich, huh? I see the bread . . . but where's the
   filling?
9. What have they got against water?
10. What have they got against ice cubes?
11. Is that why the beer is warm?
12. What this town needs is a good coffee shop.
13. What is a "stone"? How many do I weigh? How
    about *after* I eat the pork pie?

Most Brits are not very experimental about food. They won't
touch anything that they haven't eaten since earliest childhood
. . . "If Mum didn't serve it, I don't want it." This leaves them with
a very limited range, which includes toast soldiers and orange
squash. There are those who consider spaghetti bolognese and
pizza exotic . . . "foreign muck." Years spent at the mercy of Mum
and/or a succession of school cooks have made them wary of
consuming plant life (i.e., all fruit and veg.) in its natural state.
When confronted with a raw vegetable, they will revert to earliest
training and boil it for hours to make sure it is dead.

Most Yanks are heavily into food. Up to the elbows, if possible.
If they like something, they don't so much *eat* it as *merge* with it.
Basically, their tastes are simple: hamburgers, pizza, ice cream
with hot fudge. Huge, mouth-watering hunks of cheesecake
topped with whole strawberries. Also—things that remind them
of the range and variety of America's ethnic heritage—kielbasa,
strudel, lasagna, gefilte fish, pastrami. Together if possible.

As in interior decor, Yanks are open-minded about combina-
tions. After all, they invented the "combination sandwich."
(Where else can you get a corned beef, pastrami, and breast of
turkey combo, with melted cheese, coleslaw, and Russian dressing on rye?) Nevertheless, they draw the line at anything too
authentic. Culinary tradition is diverse, but carefully adapted to
American tastes . . . Yanks have a way of sanitizing food. Wiener
schnitzel may sell in a German restaurant, but not the blood
sausage. Ditto kebabs in a Greek establishment, but not the whole
baby octopus. Bland, processed "American" cheese is popular,
but the powerful French varieties virtually unknown. Though
America produces some of the world's best wines, more consumers prefer Coke.

Yanks like to be shielded from the realities of eating—and
cooking. This is, after all, the nation that invented the pop-up

I don't understand it. You've had spaghetti on toast every day for the past eighteen years.

toaster waffle and frozen orange juice. Butcher shops and super-markets are careful never to let a customer see a whole animal —nothing to associate their selections with life on the hoof. (Most Americans think that meat grows in Styrofoam and Saran wrap.) They tamper with liquor to mix the world's best cocktails —and with grain to produce the most revolting breakfast cereals. The world has Yanks to thank for sugar-coated Cocoa Puffs.

THE IMPORTANCE OF SHARING

Americans don't just *eat* food—they participate in it. Nowhere else will a total stranger pass your restaurant table, glance at your plate, and ask, "Is it good?" Eating is a shared experience. Ameri-male in love cannot take his eyes from his girlfriend's face—or his fork from her plate. True love is never having to ask permission.

Friends and relatives do the same, with a tangle of anxious arms crisscrossing the table and spearing food in all directions. Brits are put right off, seeing this as an invasion of privacy and disgusting as well. When visiting America, they live in fear that a casual acquaintance or business associate may ask to taste some-thing of theirs. Should they treat it as a presumptuous intimacy, or a friendly gesture? Does it constitute a binding contract? How can you negotiate tough terms with someone who has your hot fudge all over his face?

Because America is made for sharing, portions come in giant sizes . . . usually enough for two or three. Waitresses will provide extra plates without batting an eyelid . . . though, recently, some maverick establishments have introduced "sharing charges." These are seen as a threat to the American way of life.

In case dividing the lobster, or the spareribs, or the onion rings is messy, plastic bibs and extra napkins are provided. It is okay, even *de rigueur* in these circumstances, to behave like a slob. The waitress will eventually come around to ask if you're enjoying your dinner. It will be hard to answer with a full mouth.

American children visit restaurants from earliest infancy, and share their mothers' dinners. At the age of six, they need dinners of their own, because they eat more than she does. Brit-kids are not generally "taken out"—unless you count fast food takeouts, or the occasional tea shop treat. It is considered that they need different diets from adults, and thrive best on a meal called "nursery tea" . . . which is specially composed to include 100 percent carbohydrate, and no protein at all. Biscuits, cake, bread-and-butter, crisps, and spaghetti-on-toast are favorites. Hence, the evolution of Britain's most popular children's classics. Peter Pan was not a "lost boy" who never grew up. He was a child with protein deficiency whose growth was stunted.

BRIT GUIDE TO AMERI-PORTIONS

1. *Char-broiled New York–cut steak* (8–13 oz.)
   will overhang the plate on one side. Share with friend.
2. *Prime ribs of beef*
   will overhang the plate on both sides. Ask for *two* extra plates to take overspill.
3. *Surf-and-turf* (combo of lobster tail and steak)
   won't fit on the plate in the first place. Served on special wooden stay-hot griddle platter. You won't need dessert.
4. *Onion rings* (side order only)
   feeds four generously, six adequately. Ignore waitress's advice that you need one for every two people.
5. *Club sandwich*
   . . . not quite big enough for the whole club. Divide with one child.
6. *Salad (spinach, Waldorf, Caesar, fruit)*
   contains world's natural reserves of raw fruit and veg. Undoes benefits of low calories if you eat it all. Share with one other weight-watcher.
7. *Banana split*
   three can share. One scoop per person. Child gets the cherry.
8. *Ice cream cone (any size)*
   no one can share. It's too good, and each person will want it all. It is not unusual for a grown-up to come to blows with a child over an outstanding cone.

11
REGIONALISM AND OTHER LOCAL PROBLEMS

America has five main regions:

1. *The East*
   In theory, this means the Eastern Seaboard states. But what *really* counts is the New York City/Washington/Boston megapolitan area, combined with certain prosperous suburbs in Connecticut, White Plains, northern New Jersey, eastern Pennsylvania, Long Island, and eastern Massachusetts.
2. *The West*
   For "West," read: Greater Los Angeles, San Francisco, Marin County, Palm Springs, Scottsdale, and La Jolla. Maybe Denver, but no one knew it was there until *Dynasty.*
3. *The South*
   i.e., Atlanta, Miami, and New Orleans.
4. *Texas*
   i.e., Texas.
5. *The Midwest*
   i.e., everywhere else. For purposes of this classification, Maine is spiritually the Midwest. So is Kansas. So is Tucson. Chicago is the high spot, but because it is in the Midwest, few people yearn to live there.

Nothing which is unlisted counts, and only two of the areas above count *heavily:* 1 and 2. (Sorry, Texas.) Forget conversations you've heard about rural roots, and respect for America's heartland (i.e., the Midwest). Forget songs about going back to Swanee and midnight trains to Georgia; ditto received wisdom about the recent boom in the Sunbelt. Forget publicity about Pittsburgh being the most "livable" city in the United States, or Seattle the most beautiful. Most of all, forget comments about New York being a nice place to visit, but nobody wanting to live there. Secretly, EVERY American wants to live there—or in Los Angeles. That's why they all pack up and go there, just as soon as they grow up. Because New York and L.A. are still perceived as "best" (sorry, Texas) and the best is what every true American wants to experience. At least once. So he can say he's been.

Until a few years ago this bias toward the coasts and away from the middle (neatly summed up in the famous *New Yorker* cover) was also reflected in television programs. The vast majority used New York or L.A. as locations—notable exceptions being *Surfside 6* (Miami), *Hawaii 5-0* (Honolulu), and *The Waltons* (even if Appalachia never looked like that). Then, with *Dallas* as the groundbreaker, TV moguls discovered the allure of the regions and became more adventurous about settings . . . though choices were made with care. *Dallas* probably wouldn't've made it as *Lubbock*. *The Dukes of Hazzard,* well-situated in Jimmy Carter's Georgia, might've lost appeal in rural Alabama, or southern Missouri. Pretty soon, moguls screwed up courage to boldly go where no one but ski buffs had gone before. Denver. Whatever next . . . Wheeling? Altoona?

The point is that America's got magnets at both ends, which exert a powerful draw, and cause epic movements of peoples to opposite sides. You'd think it would droop at the edges. But Americans take the constant shifting and displacement in stride. It does not appear to provoke undue rivalry, or resentment. Sure, Californians wish midwesterners would stay out of the San Fernando Valley long enough to steady skyrocketing house prices. Okay, southerners think New York City spends extravagantly on welfare, and ought not to be bailed out with federal funds. Yes, New Yorkers with fifty-two bolts on their apartment doors taunt Texans who take a handgun when they nip down to

the 7–Eleven. (Sorry, Texas.) And certainly, there are racial
issues (like busing) which cut across regional ones. But, for the
most part, specific *regional* differences have not been a burning
obsession since Appomattox. Michigan has nothing against Ar-
kansas. And there's no question of secession for Texas. Sorry,
Texas.

───────────── B R I T - T H I N K ─────────────
Britain is, of course, much smaller in terms of area—but regional
differences are legion . . . as well as complex and occasionally
explosive (Ulster being only one manifestation). Baffled Yanks
should picture an area roughly the size of Pennsylvania, divided
into eleven distinct and potentially warring parts, some of which
threaten to secede from the rest, and from time to time shoot it
out in London. Britain is:

1. Scotland
2. Wales
3. Ulster
4. The Republic of Ireland
5. The West Country (Cornwall, Devon, Somerset)
6. The North (Manchester, Liverpool, Leeds)
7. The Northeast (Newcastle-upon-Tyne and surrounding
   economically depressed areas)
8. The Midlands (Birmingham)
9. East Anglia
10. The South (the Home Counties and similar
    commuterland)
11. Central London

Each area considers itself unique. Each feels it has certain irrecon-
cilable differences with the rest of Britain. Each lays claim to
characteristics so important and distinct that they must be:

1. acknowledged as "special" by the rest of the nation, and
2. preserved—in all their idiosyncratic glory—at any cost.

It is hard for Americans to believe, but Yorkshire and Lancashire
—which share a common border and many cultural similarities

—are hotbeds of local animosity over perceived differences. It has something to do with different recipes for Yorkshire pudding.

Curiously, for people who identify so closely with regions of origin, Brits refuse to tell outsiders where they're from. Two Yanks who meet for the first time will greet each other with "Hi. Where're you from?" "Chicago," comes the casual answer. Or "Cleveland." Nothing heavy. But try it on a Brit, and watch the harmless icebreaker cause a Big Chill. Instead of replying simply, "London," or "Manchester," he freezes, tongue-tied. You have intruded, somehow, on private matters, and embarrassed him. If he answers at all, he'll make do with an evasive "Oh, the South." Hard to come back with "Hey! I knew somebody on your street."

This reaction is hard to explain, except to say that—as ever—it has something to do with class-consciousness. Pieces of basic (and apparently neutral) data like

1. birthplace
2. father's job
3. school attended

are felt to define status, and make Brits feel exposed. Even (or especially) if your companion has a fine pedigree and an Oxbridge degree, wild horses won't drag it from him/her. Not until you know each other well. There's a ring of truth to the old joke, "Never ask an Englishman where he's from. If he's from Yorkshire, he'll tell you; and if not, it's unfair to embarrass him."

12

AT ONE WITH NATURE

Like the people, nature in Britain knows its place, and is sensibly understated. Nothing vulgar and tasteless, lavish or splashy. No great geysers or volcanos, jungles or waterfalls. Hills keep a low profile, embarrassed to be mountains, and splodge around instead camouflaged as heather-covered lumps. Nothing is out of scale. Not for rural England the extravagance of a Mt. St. Helens, or a Niagara Falls or a Grand Canyon. A Brit's idea of a canyon is when the Gas Board digs up the mains.

To Yanks, the countryside (serious, hard-core countryside) is not for *living* in (not during the week, anyway) unless you're a farmer, mountain man, or vestigial member of a hippie commune. After all, isolation can be dangerous, and self-imposed isolation is contributory negligence. Anyone who wanders too far from major urban hospitals with full medical facilities deserves what he gets.

BRIT-IDYLL

Every Brit—even if he comes from an inner-urban area like Shoreditch—is born with a deep longing for the countryside coded in his genes. This is the rural idyll. If he's forced to live and work in town, the yearning goes unsatisfied until retirement, when—seized by some primitive instinct—he "ups sticks" and moves to a seaside town he's never seen before.

Secretly, every Brit wishes he had "independent means" which would enable him to spend his whole life in the country. He sees himself as Benevolent Squire or Lord of the Manor . . . because to be landed and wellborn and own dogs and family silver and be photographed by Lichfield in a Burberry raincoat is to every Brit the apogee of existence.

Failing the whole and perfect fantasy, he settles for a reasonable approximation. He buys the raincoat. Also, a neo-Tudor home "with grounds" in a greenbelt suburb. Or a weekend country cottage, where he can live—for two days anyway—in a noncompetitive environment in contented squalor. An Englishman's compost heap is the ultimate expression of his understanding of the "quality of life."

The more unblemished his hideaway by traces of twentieth-century life (like working plumbing), the better. He and his wife will poke obsessively at innocent bits of soil for up to twelve hours a day. His crop of home-grown sprouts testifies to the fact that he is free . . . beholden to no man. He is aided and abetted by the coziness, the sheer reliability of British weather. It is sure to rain. However, he need fear no earthquakes, monsoons, hurricanes, or droughts. Even the animals are on his side (animals are *always* on a Brit's side, and vice versa). (See "Pets," p. 101.) There are virtually no poisonous snakes, no stingrays or tarantulas or rogue elephants. Statistics show that few people are savaged by sheep . . . but, in any case, sudden death seems less important when one is at one with nature. (Which is just as well, considering the caliber of rural hospitals.)

GLOSSARY OF ANGLO-AMERICAN WEATHER TERMS

AMERICAN	**BRITISH**
spring	*spring*
Three months between mid-March and mid-June when you put your winter coat away.	A time when you switch off all forms of central heating, but it remains as cold as January.
summer	*summer*
When you turn on the air conditioning.	The rain gets warmer.

AMERICAN	BRITISH
drought	*drought*
crops die. Animals in danger. Water reserves low. Dust-bowl time.	two consecutive days without downpour.
hot	*hot*
high 70s Fahrenheit, up-wards.	a glimmer of light appears be-tween cloud masses. The en-tire British nation strips to the waist. Term also describes the interior temperature of any room which has all the win-dows closed.
unbearable	*unbearable*
scorcher. 100 degrees F.	low 70s F, or more than ten minutes in the room with the windows closed.
blizzard	*blizzard*
snow drifts to several feet, traffic stops, snowplows come out. New Yorkers wear après-ski boots in streets.	slush on streets. Traffic comes to standstill. So does entire rail network.
you won't need your sweater	*you won't need your sweater*
it's T-shirt weather. Expect 80s–90s F, no rain, no wind.	no one has died of exposure overnight. (Yanks hearing this advice from a Brit should ignore it. It does not apply to them, and may be harmful to health.)
you won't need your umbrella	*you won't need your umbrella*
forecast predicts no rain. Hasn't been any for a week. Anyway, we'll be in the car.	speaker is either: (a) impersonating a Brit (True Brits never move without their brollies), or (b) no longer in Britain.

13

WHAT MAKES THIS COUNTRY GREAT?

The Very, Very Best Things in America

1. A telephone system that *works,* and has:
   (a) the same number of digits whether you're dialing Philly or Fresno, and
   (b) operators who seem to know *all* the letters in the alphabet.
2. Electrical goods sold complete with plugs, which will ll fit into any outlet in the country. Standardized screw-in lightbulbs to take the guesswork out of shopping.
3. Discount drugstores (open twenty-four hours).
4. Watchable breakfast TV.
5. The only drinkable skim milk in the world.
6. The world's best ice cream (sorry, Italians).
7. The world's best cheesecake (sorry, Germans).
8. Automatic ice water on restaurant tables.
9. Fahrenheit temperatures; inches, feet, and yards.
10. Hospital buildings that do not

The Best of British

1. A postal system that *works.* Most first-class letters arrive within twenty-four hours of posting. Delays of more than forty-eight hours are taken as evidence of social breakdown, and the government offers to resign.
2. Understanding of the restorative value of tea with milk at teatime.
3. London's black cabs. Clean, plenty of headroom, all doors convincingly attached, and drivers who know the way.
4. Wake-up alarm calls which can be booked.
5. World's cleverest shop-window displays.
6. World's best and most stylish TV commercials.
7. Milk delivered daily to the doorstep.
8. Doctors who still make house calls (offset by chemists who won't open at night or on weekends so you can fill the prescription).

increase the mortality rate by *depressing* patients to death.

11. A healthy number of medical malpractice suits, which keep doctors on their toes.

12. Washcloths in hotel bedrooms.

13. Ted Koppel, the world's best television interviewer.

14. Zillions of places where you can get it wholesale . . . whatever it is.

15. Shops and department stores that take returns without moving onto a war footing.

16. Best, cheapest, and most competitive domestic airline system in the world.

17. World's most entertaining political campaigns (money no object).

18. The existence of genuine summer.

19. Grocery shopping bags made of tough, strong paper. Supermarket packers who fill them for you, then carry them to your car.

20. Bathrooms with shower power. (Brit shower-heads are for decorative purposes only.)

21. Unleaded gas (for sale at popular prices).

22. *Hot* toast for breakfast (no toast racks) and unlimited refills on coffee.

23. Intuitive understanding of how to treat a hamburger.

24. Giant, frost-free refrigerators with ice-cube dispensers on the outside.

25. Central heating systems that mean business.

9. World's grooviest and most inventive hairdressers (pink highlights, madam?).

10. Upholstered seats in London tubes.

11. Best Italian restaurants of any city in the world, including Rome.

12. Best Indian restaurants of any city in the world, including Delhi.

13. Some of the world's best theaters, and tickets which are still cheap(ish).

14. Great bookstores, cut-price paperbacks.

15. City streets that are safe(ish).

16. The survival of the traditional British nanny (which has ensured the survival of the two-career family).

17. The only significant gay population not yet decimated by AIDS.

18. Police who, as a rule, do not carry guns, and have lots of friends who help them with their inquiries.

19. High interest rates on ordinary deposit accounts.

20. Real townhouses in the centers of big cities, some still in single-family occupation.

21. Truly prurient gossip columns appearing daily in respectable national newspapers.

22. National newspapers.

23. Public transport systems that do.

24. Preference for real wool carpet (100q) at prices which stop just short of ludicrous.

25. Wonderful parks, where civic

26. Waitresses who take an interest, and will really discuss with you whether you're going to enjoy the blintzes more with sour cream or cinnamon.

27. Sports events still attended by families, and people who have not done time for assault.

28. The ability to mix a good cocktail (this is unique on the planet).

authorities indulge the public fascination with plant life.

26. World's most beautiful traditional prams. Won't fold away and store in cars, but perfect for wheeling baby-Brits through world's most beautiful parks.

27. Appreciation of cream. Cream cakes, clotted cream teas, coffee with real cream, strawbs with cream at Wimbledon. Liquid double cream poured liberally over your already obscenely fattening fudge cake.

28. Harrod's and Harvey Nichols (where most British women would like to be forced to remain under house-arrest).

14

THE ESTABLISHMENT

Whom do Brits unreservedly love? They love entrenched members of THE ESTABLISHMENT. These are the people who have assured Brits for two generations that *Nothing Is Wrong* . . . despite all appearances to the contrary. They are, of course, society's winners; the "I'm All Right, Jack" set, with a stake in the status quo. They are fortunate in the character of the British proletariat, since average Brits are not inclined to follow malcontents with axes to grind—even when provoked, frustrated, or impoverished. They're content to allow "top people" to run the show, as long as wage packets keep rough pace with inflation, and the Clapham omnibus runs on time.

If the Establishment's track record is less than dazzling, it is nevertheless unchallenged. Brit-prol is not by nature revolutionary—or even *evolutionary*—and generally takes the view, "Better the devil you know." There's a world-weary acceptance of empires lost, opportunities unfulfilled. Would-be political agitators have ever found that Brits are civilized pessimists, given to constant recrimination—but no action. Top People are utterly safe, and can rest easy . . . if they can stand the carping.

Yanks—who lack Brit-radar—may be hard-pressed to identify members of said Establishment. By definition, these are the Chosen People at the apex of the class system. Appearances can deceive, since they may have money or may not; but what they all share is *influence.* Many were born great, some had greatness thrust upon them, and a very few achieved greatness.

Indeed, the definition is fairly vague in Brit-minds. Some refer to "the Establishment," and mean anyone who votes Tory and earns more than £20,000 a year. Some narrow it down to power brokers—people with real political clout, like captains of industry, Fleet Street proprietors, and cousins to the Queen. There are, of course, worrying gray areas. Is Bob Geldof a member of the Establishment, or not? If in doubt, try this simple litmus test:

THE BRIT-ESTABLISHMENT INCLUDES ANYONE WHO:

1. shops for basic groceries (cornflakes, bathroom cleanser) at Harrod's.
2. is regularly mentioned in *Tatler,* Dempster's column, the business pages of the *Daily Telegraph,* the *Financial Times,* and/or *Private Eye;* or has been cloned in latex by *Spitting Image.*
3. is related to the Royal Family (however distantly), had relatives who were equerries (however briefly), is a hereditary or life peer (regardless of political affiliation).
4. ever attended Oxford or Cambridge (yes, anyone).
5. sends children to private schools (day or boarding).
6. is (or whose father was) "something in the City."
7. appeared at the Live-Aid concert.
8. has an *unearned* income which tops £5,000 a year.
9. does not work, and is not in receipt of social security.
10. owns a national newspaper; has shares in—or sits on the board of—a broadcasting company.
11. has ever attended a Royal command performance of anything.
12. knows where to park in Knightsbridge.

IT DOES NOT INCLUDE SUCH INSTRUMENTS OF THE ESTABLISHMENT AS:

1. the police (they're just following instructions).
2. enlisted military men (they're just following orders).

---

3. Conservative voters of limited means (they're just following tradition).
4. taxi drivers (they're just following their instincts—and probably "that car").

In a Brit-society so cruelly divided into "winners" and "losers," they do not have a genuine stake in the winners' side.

──────── A M E R I · T H I N K ────────

In one sense, virtually *everyone* in America is THE ESTABLISH-MENT, with the possible exception of migrant workers and people on welfare. The Consensus Society is full of people with a personal stake in the system, committed to making it bigger and better, then taking a hefty cut. If you want to increase your equity (and average Yanks do), increase the market.

To this extent, trade unionists are the Establishment. Farmers and stockbrokers, artists and writers are the Establishment. In the Rambo-ized eighties, students are *certainly* the Establishment.

With political dissent virtually absent, all participants expect a piece of the action. Of course, Yanks will admit that some get a bigger piece than others . . . and, though billed as "the classless society," America has a large—and growing—Super Establishment. This is the Power Elite—the people who call the shots, who have the money and influence to make elected leaders responsive to their needs. In short, they're the ones who have it all. Here's how to recognize them:

AMERICA'S HAUTE ESTABLISHMENT—ANYONE WHO:

1. is unduly preoccupied with the latest rulings on tax shelters.
2. has stopped *buying* "how to" books and started *writing* them.
3. has ever played golf in the Bob Hope Classic.
4. buys drug items at regular price.

5. toys with the food at yet another $1,000-a-plate fund-raising dinner, then eats an omelette at home.
6. has homes and cars on both coasts.
7. is racking up "frequent traveler miles" with three separate airlines.
8. has a nutritionist, a broker, an accountant, a lawyer, a shrink, a housekeeper, and a personal "trainer," and is considering a press agent.
9. owns several furs, but spends half the year in hot climates.
10. operates a McDonald's franchise.
11. has personal and corporate AMEX Platinum Cards, and gets letters of congratulations for frequent use.
12. lost money with John DeLorean.

───── 15 ─────
GOODS AND SERVICES

Because the British feel guilty when life is too easy, Brit-consumers like—and buy—things that present a challenge. Manufacturers cater to this quirk in the national character by producing a range of products that don't entirely work. Or, sort of work. Sometimes.

Especially popular are expensive, domestically made toasters that miraculously burn bread on one side, while leaving the other side raw. This is a master stroke of mechanical and marketing genius. Brits, it seems, do not like automatic and uniformly good results. They hate being outclassed by machines, preferring to feel involved, and *necessary*. Technical perfection worries them. Given the chance, they purchase "friendly" items, which have shortcomings and need human intervention: frying pans with hard-to-reach corners that trap food; twin-tub washing machines, which require users to do half the work by hand. These give consumers a sense of purpose.

Many Brits are not at one with science. They are skeptical about modern technology, and feel gratified when doubts are confirmed by experience. Mechanical fallibility restores their faith in human beings, their love for nature, and gives them a chance to laugh at those who overreach themselves by inventing smart gadgets. Brits are so relieved and have such a chuckle when things go wrong.

Ad agencies take careful note of such reactions, and time after time produce brilliant campaigns, admirably tailored to Brit-psyches. In brief, it's the classic British undersell, and products

must be portrayed as short on technology, long on natural goodness (and/or connection with the countryside). Ads for a new cake mix never claim "perfect results every time!" This rules out the possibility of failure, and does not underscore the importance of the human contribution or the "naturalness" of the product. Far better, "perfect country cakes, nine times out of ten!" Know thy customer. It'll sell and sell.

In any case, Brits are perverse enough to shun goods that are the subject of extravagant claims. They pride themselves on being too smart to fall for hype. They do not rush—as Yanks do —to buy "the best/the brightest/the softest" item on the market, preferring a low-key approach. "Dazzle—not bad for a fabric whitener" makes them love the product. It has so little to live up to. And consumer criticism is utterly defused by the clever "British Rail . . . We're Getting There."

CONSPICUOUS CONSUMPTION

———————— A M E R I - S T Y L E ————————

Americans are quite simply the best consumers in the world . . . the most enthusiastic and experienced. They'll consume carefully or conspicuously, but consume they must—and on a regular basis. No wonder a famous American T-shirt reads, "Whoever Has the Most Things When He Dies Wins." Yanks —indisputably the best-equipped people in the world—hedge constantly against the possibility of shortage. They seem to need a lot of stuff. That's why, when they find something they like, they buy "in multiples"—i.e., several of the same thing in different colors. They do this with Lacoste sports shirts featuring an alligator on the front. They do it with cashmere sweaters and leather loafers. When in doubt, Yanks will always purchase, on the grounds that it never hurts to have another one of anything, but you may be sorry *not* to. They are the only people in the world overheard reassuring each other in department stores, "Buy, buy. So you'll *have* an extra raincoat."

Yanks are also the most *receptive* consumers on earth. Brits may think them credulous and gullible, but the truth is that they *believe* in products. First of all, they are culturally predisposed to think that "new is good," and "newer is better." Hooked on the idea of progress and growth, they're convinced that the quality of life is susceptible to all kinds of improvement. Hence, they embrace technological (if not political) change. There's an underlying assumption that research solves problems . . . and you, too, can benefit from the latest developments.

It follows that Yanks love the word *now*. "Crunchie's Cornflakes—*now* fortified with iron"; "aspirin . . . *now* coated for stomach protection"; "diet cola—*now* 97 percent caffeine-free". Copywriters know that the word can boost sales by up to 25 percent. There's public confidence that, if someone bothered to change it, they must've made it better.

SELLING OUT

——————— A M E R I - S E L L ———————

British and American sales personnel are present in stores for entirely different reasons. Yanks are there to increase their take-home pay by making commissions on sales. In this, they are helped by their store's inventory policy. Let's take women's fashions. If a customer sees something she likes, chances are that it can be found in stock in her size, her color. *If not,* it can be located at a nearby branch, and sent to her branch free of charge. *If not,* her branch will "special order" her choice direct from the manufacturer. One way or another, the salesperson will get the item and make the sale, even if she has to walk to the warehouse. After all—she has 3 percent riding on it.

BRIT-SELL

British salespeople are very attached to merchandise and try hard to keep it in the store. They will not part with goods unless forced. For example, if you ask for a particular size, they will:

1. ignore you.
2. point in the direction of a rack across the floor, without breaking off their conversation long enough to acknowledge you.
3. snap, "If it's not out, we haven't got it."

If you positively *insist* on buying something, the in-store system will force you to queue for ages at a crowded till in order to pay for it. They'll take even longer to okay the purchase on your credit card, so as to discourage you for next time. And they will never, *ever* agree to refund or credit anything, unless threatened with the full weight of the law. Brit salespeople believe in strong deterrents for recidivist shoppers . . . and they make sure that the punishment fits the purchase. They are visibly relieved if you just go away. They're not, after all, there to sell. They are there to talk with colleagues about last night's date, and you are bothering them.

BRIT-SHOP

Brits are somewhat oppressed—even intimidated—by salespeople, and tend to shop apologetically. They don't like to be trouble to anyone: "Awfully sorry to bother you . . . do you have this in a size eight?" Men suffer particularly from shop/phobia, and will do anything to avoid contact—never mind confrontation. They are obedient and inhibited customers. In shops, they rush to purchase the first garment or pair of shoes produced, and hate asking to try other sizes or styles. They shop only when forced by circumstances, and never for pleasure. They are pushovers as consumers, since they will buy *anything*—literally—just to get out of the store.

Brits are mortally embarrassed by salespeople. This is because, being polite people, they have never learned how to say no to them. They buy things they don't want because they lack the finesse required to extricate themselves from situations. And, since they *know* they'll be trapped, they avoid entering shops altogether. Even normally dynamic Brits are utterly compliant customers . . . putty in the hands of Marks & Spencer's most junior assistant. Their mouths cannot form the crucial series of one-syllable words, "No-thanks-I-don't-like-it." Salespeople know this and exploit the advantage . . . taking Brit-consumer's money, secure in the knowledge that they'll never, ever be asked to give it back.

──────────── A M E R I - S H O P ────────────

Yanks, as the world's most dedicated consumers, sport a series of shopping-related badges and bumper stickers that read:

1. WHEN THE GOING GETS TOUGH, THE TOUGH GO SHOPPING.
2. WHO SHOPS WINS.
3. IF YOU THINK MONEY CAN'T BUY HAPPINESS, YOU'VE BEEN SHOPPING IN THE WRONG PLACES.
4. SHOPPING IS MY EVEREST.
5. MORE IS MORE.

There is nothing more satisfying to them than the sense of achievement and *control* that comes with Purchase Power. There is nothing so gratifying as a good fight in a store—which they inevitably win, since America's customer is always right. American women fight for recreation in Saks much as they play tennis or visit museums.

They have no psychological problem with salespeople, who are there to serve. They address them without embarrassment, since, in America, everyone's selling something anyway. Yes, everyone shops, and shopping is the Great Equalizer. It's the Consensus Society extended to the Consumer Society.

For Yanks, shopping also has a healing and therapeutic effect. Shops are where you fantasize about the future and try it on for size. They're where you put the present together, a piece at a time. If life is about Having It All, shops are where you get It. But, most important of all, shopping is about *control* . . . i.e., if it's my money, I get to get what I want. Including the treatment I think I deserve. Stores are places where money puts *you* in charge, and you can make sure you get what's coming to you. When you shop, you should ideally purchase victory. It's good for the soul.

16

PETS

Household pets have long been popular in both Britain and America . . . playthings for affluent societies. Nonworking animals that have to be fed remain luxuries for the relatively rich (not many poodles in Ethiopia) and whole menageries are for the relatively richer. Private zoos and safari parks exist all over Britain, and in some parts of Hollywood (where there are lots of animals).

For Anglo-American animal lovers, pets are diversions and objects of affection. They are also fashion accessories that say as much about an owner's style and aspirations as the clothes he/she wears, the books read, the music listened to. Speak, Rover.

That is why, without question, *dogs* are man's best friend. It's said that elderly ladies prefer cats, that rock stars take iguanas for walks on leashes and sailors talk most openly to parrots. But dogs most nearly reflect and then *project* their owners' personalities. Both Brit and Yank owners know precisely how to "say it with Rover."

AMERI-POOCH

. . . is the best friend of a conspicuous consumer. Time was ('round about the fifties) when Yanks in the fast lane just *had* to have poodles. Budding starlets walked them on Hollywood Boulevard, where it was chicer still to dye them pink. The color matched your outfit, your bedroom, or your eyes, and demonstrated to the world that you were successful enough to afford the grooming charges.

Today, virtually any pooch can complete your image, or tell

your story. You're free to walk a Schnauzer or a Great Dane or a Shi Tzu with a bow in its hair. Even a friendly mutt with one white-ringed eye and a floppy ear says much about your casual, blue-denim style.

Just as telling are the *names* Americans give their pets. "Ralph" to suggest the unpretentious mongrel found in an alleyway; "Spago" for a Beverly Hills pup, named after the town's grooviest restaurant; "Bismarck" for a dachshund with an educated owner.

Yanks who want to Have It All do not cut corners when it comes to Rover. They'll go all out on poodle parlors with pet saunas and herbal baths, or top vets with high-tech offices . . . offering laser treatment, vitamins, plastic surgery (ears pinned back for a self-conscious cocker), and doggie TV featuring remote-control channel-changer ("he just loves *Dynasty,* and we never watch it").

. . . And, yes, doggie psychiatry. Barry Manilow really did have his beagle, Bagel, analyzed.

Ameri-pet may even carry the burden of his owner's fantasies. Some Yanks enjoy casting their pets as heroes, sort of furry four-legged Clint Eastwoods or Charles Bronsons (who is pretty furry already). Hence the popularity of Lassie, Rin Tin Tin and Rex the Wonder Dog. It's not enough for Ameri-dog merely to lick his owner, and chew on an old slipper. He's also got to save the world.

BRIT - DOG

. . . has one major aspirational function. This is to help his owner to live out the "Country Life" fantasy, which suggests sprawling estates with people in tweeds and plenty of animals. Brit-pooch is the "plenty of animals." (This is no mean achievement when you live in a basement flat in Putney.) Nothing daunted, Brit-owner will don woolens and Wellies for a walk with Fido across open heath (or failing that, a grass verge will do), emerging at the corner Indian grocery for a pint of milk. Fido does his bit by barking away, pretending to be a brace of dogs on a double lead, hot on the scent of something countrified . . . but spoils the illusion by sniffing at every Mars Bar wrapper on the pavement.

Brit-dog has few luxuries in this life, like grooming parlors and gourmet dinners. No one follows him around with a gold-plated Pooper-Scooper; he's lucky if he's had his injections, and been dewormed. He certainly doesn't boast a poncey name, and is likely to answer to "Blackie" or "Spot" or "Tim." But his owner loves him (often better than people), and lets him chew on scraps of fresh rabbit, and likes it best when he shakes them all over the quarry-tiled floor of the kitchen, because it conjures up visions of great liver-colored dogs in great stone-floored halls near great hearths on great country estates far, far from Balham.

Brit-dog is not hero; he is *hunter*. His owner likes to dream of him following a carefully laid aniseed trail, or savaging a fox. (In fact, he is more likely to savage a soft ginger biscuit, or the family cat.) Brits also adore sheepdogs. Britain is probably the only country on earth which could run TV sheepdog trials in prime time, and get soap-sized ratings. What Joan Collins is to Yanks' fantasies, sheepdogs are to Brits'.

17
JUDGING A NATION BY ITS TELEVISION

MEET THE PRESS

It's always dangerous to make snap judgments about someone else's television. Brits criticize the American product for being intellectually negligible and crass; Yanks regard much U.K. output as slow, worthy, and turgid. But prolonged TV viewing is a wonderful key to national attitudes.

It should be said that although we feel we are well-acquainted with each other's TV, we are not. Most Brits base their opinions of America's vast news and entertainment offerings on:

1. imports screened in the U.K., and
2. a few hours of sporadic viewing at a motel near the L.A. airport.

Similarly, Yanks form impressions of Brit-progs by dipping in and out of the (intellectually rarefied) PBS network. When in London, they may catch a special on *Birds of Britain*, or *One Man and His Dog*, in prime time. These are not regarded as compulsive viewing. Then, after 1:30 A.M., all is darkness.

———————————— A M E R I - T V ————————————

First, there's lots of it. Americans believe in superabundant choice, and see no reason why TV should be an exception to the rule. Second (and as a result), it is competitive . . . with dozens of channels chasing a limited—if large—number of viewers. Success depends on attracting attention. Programs need to make a splash; ditto personalities. (In a country with 230 million people, you can't be quiet and expect the culture to recognize you.)

So: The first ninety seconds of your station's new sit-com must be the freshest, the funniest, the sexiest. A cops 'n' robbers series had better be the most thrilling and dangerous, with nary a wasted frame. Girls must be pretty. Men must be handsome. Ameri-audiences have learned to expect instant gratification, and there are no second chances. Even producers of high-quality current affairs are at pains to satisfy popular tastes. Disappoint the viewer, and other worlds are his at the touch of a remote-control button: from feature films on cable, to MTV, twenty-four-hour news, soft porn, or reruns of *Mork and Mindy.* This is the video equivalent of Having It All. The result is that makers of American television have created rods for their own backs by creating Ameri-viewer. Overstimulated, restless, and skittish, he typically has the attention span of an ant (research shows a maximum of three minutes). His ability to concentrate is shot.

―――――――――― B R I T - T E L L Y ――――――――――

Brits confuse TV in general (and the BBC in particular) with morality in general and goodness in particular. They are never sure where entertainment fits in, let alone commerce . . . and

Zap, Zap, Zap! To say you had the attention span of an ant would be insulting to ants.

grapple hopelessly with these issues every time the license fee comes up for renewal.

To resolve the confusion, they have set up "watchdog" bodies (rough equivalents to America's FCC) to monitor broadcasting and make sure that no one enjoys it too much. Part of their job is to limit competition (i.e., the number of stations on the air) and to interfere as much as possible with the ones they've got. As a result, no one knows whether British TV is:

1. a branch of government and/or the Home Office.
2. electronic Moral Example (a branch of the Church of England).
3. just another means of selling toothpaste.
4. an adventure playground for "creative" adults (e.g., journalists and producers) who would be a nuisance and virtually unemployable elsewhere.

Brit-TV executives pride themselves on intellectual and creative integrity. They are, they claim, above the ignoble American scramble for ratings. They do not pander to viewers accustomed to "instant nirvana," and are fully prepared to give new programs a chance to "run in." Nor are they slaves to the sudden-death ratings system known as "overnights." (They can't *afford* overnights.) Success, they claim, is not about "popularity." In truth, they see program content as some reflection of the quality of their own minds and do not wish to be judged harshly. This presents problems when considering *Game for a Laugh*.

But what really annoys Brit-TV moguls is the thought that "formula" American programs—often high on lip-gloss and low on IQ— have consistently swept the boards in Britain. Brit-viewer (accustomed as he is to Finer Things) has not proved immune to the charm of *Charlie's Angels*. This seems like a betrayal, but does nothing to *change* (there's that word again) programming policy. It merely proves that viewer flesh is contemptibly weak. Also, that Yanks have mastered the trick of producing images and stories deeply satisfying to a broad public (no mean achievement). Brit-moguls could, of course, refuse to *buy* them; but that would be commercial suicide. Instead, they compromise by showing them and being snooty about them at the same time. Brit-viewers, for their part, have rapidly acquired more videocassette recorders per capita than any other country in the world except Japan, and use them to watch American films.

YOU ARE WHAT YOU WATCH
——————— A M E R I - V I S I O N ———————
Yanks have few philosophical problems with television. They have more or less resolved the conundrum about combining hard news investigation with ads for Toyotas. At bottom, they're confident that program *quantity* finally ensures fairness and quality . . . and this is a safety net. If the "ignoble scramble for ratings" produces some dire daytime soaps and pretty thin sitcoms, it's also brought us *M*A*S*H** and *Sergenat Bilko,* and Ted Koppel and Edward R. Murrow. Most important, Yanks see television as a business first of all, and a public utility second. No network presumes to appoint itself guardian of public morals and arbiter of taste. That's *your* job.

THEY'RE WATCHING ME
——————————— B R I T - T V ———————————
Brit program-makers are often hampered in their jobs by the Brit Establishment's (see Chapter 14) photophobia. Power brokers (politicians apart) often regard the camera as the enemy, and do not like being watched. The impact of pictures transmitted direct to the public is random, dangerous . . . impossible to judge. Where possible, the Great British Public is prohibited from receiving its information "neat." So, cameras are excluded from

1. courts of law. (Reporters are compelled to *sketch* pictures of the proceedings instead.)
2. the House of Commons. (Where necessary, the nightly news shows slides of MPs—or the debating chamber—combined with audio recordings.)

3. wars. (When Brit-troops engaged the Argies in the Falklands, reporters were asked to leave their cameras at home.)

YANKS ON VIDEO

Yanks love cameras, and basically feel that *nothing is real* unless it exists on video. I Vide(o), Therefore I Am. Andy Warhol struck an all-American chord when he predicted that in the future, everyone would be world-famous for fifteen minutes. The press has instant access to events and people, with only the inner recesses of the Pentagon and the CIA generally off-limits. This can lead to press scrimmages and the abandonment of all acceptable standards of behavior when the heat is on (witness the TWA Beirut hostage crisis). On the plus side, it has also led to Watergate, and to demands for the present Freedom of Information Act, which increases the government's accountability to Ameripublic. TV transforms reality.

—— 18 ——
HUMOR TRAVELS?

TRANSATLANTIC LAUGHS

When two countries share a common language it is easy to assume that they also share the attitudes and points-of-reference which are the basic stuff of humor. Yanks and Brits really don't. If proof is needed, remember initial Ameri-bafflement at things Pythonesque. Or how edited highlights of the vastly popular *Tonight* show with Johnny Carson laid a U.K. egg.

There are, of course, successes as well, which explains the frequent cross-fertilization of TV programs; but choices must be made with care. Some things won't travel. A Brit trying his favorite Rik Mayall impression on a Yank should prepare for a blank stare. And American comedienne Joan Rivers leaves her favorite "K mart" jokes out of all her U.K. routines. The point is that when your plane leaves London Heathrow Airport or JFK, you leave behind a whole series of cultural references, too.

———— A M E R I - L A U G H S ————

American humor is about stand-up comics, rooted in vaudeville and aspiring to Vegas (or a spot on the Carson show) with a series of quick-fire gags and one-liners. "New wave" comics are those who start out at the *Comedy Store* or similarly, before moving to Vegas and the Carson show by way of *Saturday Night Live.*

But the influence of the "Greats"—George Burns, Jack Benny —remains. The best (and most exportable) American sit-coms are a collection of high-quality laugh-lines bedded in the matrix of a story *(M*A*S*H*, Rhoda, Cheers)*. The most popular funny films feature the likes of Eddie Murphy or Woody Allen, firing gags just as appropriate to the midnight show at Caesar's Palace: "That's my ex-wife . . . I almost didn't recognize her without her wrists cut." Or: "Hollywood's so clean! No garbage in the streets—because they put it all on television." Or: "Been to Beverly Hills? They're so rich, they watch *Dynasty* to see how *poor* people live. They're so rich, the 7-Eleven has a fur department." Or (in *Annie Hall*): "Nice parking. I can walk to the curb from here."

To be funny in America, you have to be:
1. a member of an ethnic minority. There are no such things as "WASP" jokes—unless a Jewish comedian tells them.
2. from a large urban area, and (preferably) a deprived background. The skepticism which is the leitmotiv of Ameri-comedy is honed in adversity, which is the same as Brooklyn.
3. a natural cynic, with a tendency toward paranoia. (If you've suffered at the hands of the American medical profession, so much the better.) Life's a mess, human motivation is base, and they're all out to get you anyway. Classic Ameri-comic sees himself as the long-suffering, hard-pressed realist (Jackie Mason, Lennie Bruce, Mort Sahl, Bob Hope) . . . the last bastion of sanity in a flakey world, knowing the score, telling it "like it is," keeping his head when, all around him, shnooks are losing theirs. "I met a guy the other day . . . wife's left him, he's got no money and no job. But he's *happy*. Know why? Stupid."

———————— B R I T - L A U G H S ————————

Modern British humor also derives from the music hall—which is the rough equivalent of vaudeville. It, too, is urban in outlook . . . though only *specific* urban areas will do. People from northern cities like Manchester and Liverpool are funny, because the alternative is suicidal despair. (In some northern towns, suicide is redundant.) Rural areas do not generate humor (Brits take the countryside too seriously) and Chipping Sodbury has produced few great comics.

Londoners can be funny, but only if they're from the East End —with the chirpy, street-smart, wide-boy sense of humor which that implies. You can poke fun *at* people who come from NW3, or Islington, or Surbiton. No one funny has ever come from Twickenham, Croydon, or Friern Barnet . . . though comedians from the East End who have made money hurry to live there.

To be funny in Britain, you have to:
1. portray yourself as a loser and nitwit. It is *you* who are out of step with the rest of society, *you* who march to the beat of a different drummer. Brit-comic often plays the nerd, or the loony. Classic example is John Cleese as Basil Fawlty; or Morecambe and Wise, vying with each other to see who is the bigger nincompoop. Ditto the Two Ronnies, or Pete and Dud . . . the unself-consciously hopeless, pitted against a world which is basically sane. Then came Python, in which the world *and* the people in it were mad, and followed to the letter the logic of their own lunacy: summarize-Proust competitions and parrot sketches, and

   "Buried the cat last week."
   "Was it dead?"
   "No, we just didn't like it very much."
2. be brave about death. (Yank-comics won't touch it with a barge pole . . . and Ameri-audiences don't believe in it anyway.) But north of Watford, the sense of humor is sub-fusc black. Nothing raises a bigger laugh than a good death or funeral joke:

   DOCTOR: You're in great shape. You'll live to be ninety.
   PATIENT: I *am* ninety.
   DOCTOR: Oh, well. That's it, then.

Even Python raised its biggest laugh with a sketch about an ex-parrot that had gone to meet its Maker and was nailed to its perch.

3. neutralize female sexuality. Women are not the air-headed, full-bosomed sex objects of Ameri-comedy, but more often the beefy and relentless predators who come between men and their preferred pursuits. Red-blooded northern males would rather be down "at t'pub," or playing darts with "t'lads," while leaving the little woman to exhaust her libido by mending the roof on the garden shed. The north is a Man's World. And when death finally comes to claim the menfolk, northern women can scarcely tell the difference.

There's one more quirk about Anglo-American humor. It has to do with *which* ethnic or regional groups are perceived as figures of fun. Yanks tell Polish jokes, while Brits—who never knew that Poles were especially hopeless—enjoy Irish jokes. They'll also send up Aussies ("Mind if I call you Bruce, Bruce?") or people from Neasden ("Neasditz"), but haven't hooked into the whole idiom of "Californian" jokes. Example:

> QUESTION: How many Californians does it take to change a light bulb?
> ANSWER: Twelve. One to screw it in, and eleven to share the experience.

OR:

> QUESTION: What's Californian for "Boy, am I ever gonna screw you up"?
> ANSWER: "Trust me, trust me."

— 19 —
GOOD SPORT

PLAYING TO WIN

It's not "how you play the game," no sirree, Bob. It's whether you win or lose. Even more important, it's how you *pay* the game. Professional sportsmen and sportswomen have careers that are nasty, brutish, and short, so they've a right to pocket what they can while they're young and hot.

Sport in America is three things:

1. another branch of show-biz.
2. a ritualized exercise in patriotism and regional loyalty— i.e., a way of saying, "My country is better than your country," and "Cleveland is better than Cincinnati."
3. a branch of the Bank of America—i.e., a commercial bonanza for athletes, sponsors, and promoters.

FAIR PLAY

Brits are respected the world over for the quality of their sportsmanship, and sense of fair play. They are also known for their fondness for amateurism, reluctance to invest in sport, and lack of organized, up-to-date training facilities. This means that Brit-athletes are somewhat hampered, and tend to compete with one set of pectorals tied behind their backs. Internationally, at least, they seldom win anything . . . which they put down to a superior sense of fair play. (Fair play does not extend to Brit-fans' treatment of the other team's supporters, which is more like foul play.)

Brits have great patience in sport. That's why they invented cricket, which is an exercise of such subtlety that only life-long devotees can tell when the ball is actually in play. The moment of maximum spectator appeal comes when players break for tea. Otherwise, games can continue for two or three days with no clear result. Ditto snooker, which lacks the excitement of jai alai, downhill racing, or the roller derby, but keeps Brit-audiences glued to tellies in huge numbers for days at a time.

Both Britain and America have "national" sports (cricket and baseball), which are played in the summer, and get smaller gates than various versions of football (played in the winter), which attract bumper crowds.

AMERICAN FOOTBALL IS:

1. a contact sport for those who also enjoy watching head-on collisions between Refrigerators,
2. at college level, a means of awarding athletic scholarships to fellows who count best if it's in yard lines, and
3. at the professional level, an excuse for patriotic displays at halftime, postgame parties, and mega-salaries for anyone who looks like Joe Namath.

BRIT-FOOTIE IS:

1. a means of social mobility, whereby working-class lads— with no other options save jobs down the pits or in rock bands—can earn a decent living while preserving lungs and eardrums, and
2. a way of letting off steam in public, allowing Brit-fans to pummel one another to a pulp in the stands while players hug and kiss on the field.

—— 20 ——
WAR GAMES

In spite of the fact that the U.S. is arguably the most powerful nation in the world, Yanks are not a warlike people. America was founded by pacifist religious groups who had broken ties with Europe, and the legacy remains. Throughout their short history Americans have formulated or signed many policy documents meant to reduce the possibility of conflict: i.e., the League of Nations Charter, the Monroe Doctrine, the present U.N. Charter, and the Marshall Plan. They have entered both world wars late, and with considerable reluctance. In the sixties, America made Peace and Love fashionable; and by the early seventies, aversion to war was so widespread that Nixon was forced to extricate America from Vietnam. Yes, average Americans hate fighting . . . yet, they are perceived by others as a trigger-happy and hawkish nation. This is because:

1. They are the world's foremost nuclear power (Might makes Fright).
2. They once "nuked" Japan.
3. They're moving further to the political right, in pursuit of
4. a hardline Republican president who is not crazy about Communists but loves cowboy novels.
5. The successful development of Star Wars could shift the balance of power and leave the U.S. holding the nuclear trump card.
6. Yanks may not like fighting foreign wars, but they carry guns and spend a lot of time shooting each other.

7. They fight wars in third-world countries by proxy, using CIA operatives with slush funds instead of military troops.
8. In matters of foreign policy, they have been known to support right-wing regimes that seem to prefer genocide to Communism.
9. They are fully committed to the American Way of Life, and have scant time or tolerance for alternative points of view; and, more important,
10. they have 45,000 nuclear warheads, and will not put hands on hearts and promise not to use them.

―――――――――― B R I T - T H I N K ――――――――――

Brits see themselves as a well-behaved people, peace-loving and slow to anger. In fact, they have seldom said no to a good war. They entered with great spirit into the Battle of the Armada, the Hundred Years War, the Wars of the Roses (they have ever been keen gardeners), and any number of colonial wars. They were quick off the mark in the First and Second World Wars, and more recently dispatched a task force to the Falklands at the first sign of Argie provocation. Mrs. T. proclaimed herself "miffed" at America for invading Grenada, but was happy to send ten times as many troops ten times as far from home, to defend one-tenth the number of civilians and around ten times as many sheep.

Britain has recently entered a period of heightened anti-American feeling, triggered by the deployment of U.S. cruise missiles in Europe. This mood of antagonism is thought to owe much to successful lobbying by the British peace movement for unilateral disarmament. The analysis is not entirely correct. It's true that large numbers of Brits (especially young and politically liberal ones) object to an American military presence in the U.K. As an extension of that, more general resentment and mistrust of all things American are commonplace. But it does not follow that average Brits reject nuclear warfare, embrace peace, or hate bombs. Evidence suggests that they would simply prefer *British* bombs.

Many Brits now realize that they would have done well to

follow de Gaulle's example. His nuclear strategy was essentially "France for the French." He insisted upon domestically made bombs ("French fission"), an independent deterrent, and independent defense. Today, les Frogs are reliable NATO partners and *contents comme tout* (happy as sandboys), while Brits feel hijacked by the Americans, agonize endlessly about "dual key," and worry about ending up as a medium-range atomic sacrifice in the clash of the Titans.

— 21 —
RELIGIOUS PERSUASIONS

BORN (AGAIN) IN THE U.S.A.

─────────── A M E R I - T H I N K ───────────

America was founded by religious dissenters seeking freedom of
worship, and is still a haven for virtually any group, subscribing
to any set of beliefs . . . however loony. If you wish to find karma
by worshiping sunflowers in the nude while chewing betel nuts
and giving all your money to an El Dorado–driving Oriental,
California has a place for you. This implies that America is a
diverse and religiously tolerant nation, which is not strictly true,
since in certain parts of the South they beat you up if you don't
believe in Jesus.

Presidential candidates from all political parties must show
themselves to be both God-fearing and churchgoing, so as not
to alienate the Moral Majority, the Silent Majority, or even plain
ol' Middle America. Urban-based, Yuppie-supported liberal
Democrats are stuck with the greatest dilemma, since the demands of a national campaign will force them to abandon principles and renounce "abortion on demand" if they want to get
elected . . . witness Geraldine Ferraro's desperate compromise:
"I wouldn't choose it for myself, but I believe that all women
should have the option." Nice try. Look where it got her.

Amazing footwork is required in order to curry favor with all
disparate religious groups while antagonizing none. Victory to
the greatest dancer. Hopefuls must eat bagels and lox with the
Jewish community in Brooklyn, then fly off for gravlax with
Lutherans in Minnesota. They must chew the fat with Irish Cath-

olics in Boston, expressing opposition to the British presence in Northern Ireland, while deftly sidestepping promises of support for the IRA. Not to mention the ERA. God knows, it is not easy.

However, all religious groups in the United States have one thing in common: devotion to fund-raising. In the same way that patriotism merges with show biz, Ameri-religion is tied up with cash; and it is no news to anyone that God is Big Business. The South is awash with video ministers . . . influential Fundamentalists who buy TV airtime in order to evangelize on an epic scale. It's a sort of satellite feed of the faithful. And the faithful respond by donating (tax-deductible) millions. Such is the level of American giving that Yanks have discovered a crossover point between charity and world domination. Did funds contributed in the United States to NORAID buy the IRA bomb which very nearly wiped out Mrs. Thatcher and her Cabinet at Brighton? Did American Sikhs, at present underwriting the rebuilding of the Golden Temple at Amritsar, also engineer the assassination of Mrs. Gandhi? And to what extent is conflict in the Middle East sustained by interest groups Stateside? Who needs the State Department when you can make your own policy at fund-raising dinners, over the chicken-and-lobster in a patty shell.

BRIT-THINK

Britain is probably the most irreligious nation on earth, which many feel is its great attraction. It is possible to live in some parts of England for years and never meet anyone who regularly attends a place of worship. Most Brits will say, if pressed, that they are "C. of E." . . . but reserve the right to do nothing about it. Lack of high-profile—and highly commercialized—religious fervor is one of the more remarkable things about the nation and may explain much of its political stability.

As ever, Brits mistrust the emotionally charged, the irrational. They have before them the chastening example of Ireland/Ulster. That way lies madness, which, in any case, is endemic in devout, sectarian countries where people are constantly bashing each other up in the name of God. Look at Spain, France, and Italy. The Middle East doesn't bear thinking about. And in the

Republic of Ireland and Ulster—the only parts of the U.K. where religion is a burning issue—there's an orgy of bloodletting, with loony pitted against loony.

No: so far as most Brits are concerned, religious affiliation is a private matter . . . slightly embarrassing, like name-of-hometown-and-father's-occupation. It's about obligingly putting on hats to go to weddings, christenings, and funerals. Period. Religion should not be allowed to change your way of life, much less deplete your bank account. A few coins in the plate are fine when the church roof has dry rot, but splashy contributions are not called for. Brit-religion has no grandiose, international vision. That's Bob Geldof's job. Anyway—charitable donations are not tax-deductible.

─── 22 ───
THE GOLDEN YEARS ...
LIFE BEGINS AT SIXTY

GIVING IN GRACEFULLY

─────────── B R I T - T H I N K ───────────

People should not try too hard to hold back the ravages of time. Face-lifts and jogging geriatrics are vaguely obscene. One should grow old gracefully, bow to the inevitable . . . (be content to look dreadful). It's ghastly and unnatural to throw it about like Joan Collins. All older women (anyone past fifty) should choose as a role model for dress and decorum the Queen Mum. The Queen certainly has.

Any Brit over sixty-five, regardless of financial circumstances, rejoices in the title of "old-age pensioner"—abbreviated to OAP. The label is designed to depress him to death quickly, thus saving money for the State. In order to help speed the elderly on their way, Brits have devised a State Pension Scheme that gives a whole new meaning to the word *subsistence,* and ensures that the vast majority of OAPs live in genuine poverty. The financial arrangements made for them by the State are predicated on the idea that, as you get older, your system slows down, so you don't need to eat.

Many impoverished OAPs have the decency to retreat to damp and gloomy basement flats where no one sees them (until a caring milkman, alerted by souring pints on the doorstep, pronounces them dead). Meanwhile, they can make endless cups of tea and huddle by paraffin fires, which is what old people

enjoy. For an occasional treat, they open a tin of salmon or
hobble down to the post office. On a good day they catch a
glimpse of that lovely Princess Diana on the telly. The sight of
privileged young Royals spreading themselves around always
bucks old people up.

I HAVE NOT YET BEGUN TO FIGHT

———————— A M E R I - T H I N K ————————

Death is optional. Or may be. At any rate, no point in lying down
until you're dead. You owe it to yourself to maintain life at peak
quality for as long as possible. If this means face-lifts or eyelid
surgery or hair transplants or four expensive weeks at the Priti-
kin Institute for Longevity . . . go for it. If it means a new fur
coat, which simply makes you *feel* as if you'll live longer, then
that's okay, too.

America's "pensioners" are not automatically perceived as
vulnerable and poor. The euphemistic phrase "senior citizen"
(Yanks won't tolerate anything less positive) calls to U.S. minds
a healthy older person in modest but comfortable circumstances.
A lifetime of conscientious work has now made possible a Florida
apartment, paid-up medical insurance, and regular long-distance
phone calls to children and grandchildren in other cities.
His/her reward in the skies (if not in heaven) is a special senior
citizens' rate on cross-country air travel.

Ameri-pensioners in most social categories are obsessed by
fitness and health. Naturally. It stands to reason that you have to
take care of yourself if you're going to last. Observe on any
Ameri-beach the jogging octogenarian, tanned to a deep shade
of prune, and pausing only to pop a fistful of vitamin B-complex
and yeast. He stopped smoking twenty years ago and is now busy
cutting all fats from his diet . . . "keep the old arteries clean and
you don't get senile." He has cornered the world market in skim
milk, virtually eliminated red meat, takes the skin off chicken,
and adds no butter to his steamed vegetables or morning whole-
grain toast. He won't eat a pretzel without scraping the salt off
first. His greatest fear in life is being caught somewhere where

———————————————————————————————

you can't get dental floss. He can reel off the name of virtually every carcinogen known to modern medicine, in between mouthfuls of bran. He sees life as a minefield of potential hazards for the elderly, which—with determination—he can sidestep. Avoid getting zapped, and the prize is—who knows?—immortality! Sound crazy? Well, there are no guarantees in this life, and until someone comes up with a better theory, he's sticking to the one he's got.

23

WHAT *REALLY* COUNTS

If there's one thing that True Brits have, it's a sense of priorities.
When all is said and done, only *two things* really count; and—
singly or together—they are the quintessence of Brit-life:

1. *The Royal Family*
   . . . beloved of everyone—even the long-term
   unemployed and "hard-line" socialists, who would gladly
   smash the system, but leave intact every hair and ostrich
   feather on the Queen Mum's head. The Royals *are*
   Britain. They're WHAT WE'RE ABOUT, and DUTY,
   and HOW WE DO THINGS, and WE'VE ALWAYS
   DONE IT THIS WAY . . . a diamond-studded bulwark
   against any form of social change. Ever.
       They are contentment . . . human incarnations of
   qualities and spiritual values that transcend hard cash.
   Royals inhabit a Higher Plane, since they are so rich that
   they need never concern themselves about money. Brits
   draw comfort from that.

2. *The Pub*
   . . . focal point of Brit-life, the Great Leveler (the *only*
   leveler) that unites dustmen and kings. Pubs are
   comfortable and comforting—places where average Brits
   can rehearse cozy thoughts and attitudes, sure of
   endorsement and a sympathetic hearing from others too
   smashed to notice.
       Brits make it through a working morning only by

looking forward to drinking lunch in the nearest pub, then remain groggy for most of the working afternoon, surfacing just in time to grab a "quick one" at 6 P.M. before starting for home and an evening's telly, followed by a nip down to the local for "last orders" at eleven . . . which ensures the residual hangover that dulls work performance the next morning until it's time to break for a pub lunch—and so on.

In pubs, Brits put problems to rights, reassure everyone about everything, blow all surplus cash, and escape the pressures of family life for a glorious hour or two. Pubs are "public" in the true sense of the word, since women on their own, or gaggles of "girlfriends," or OAPs are welcome, as long as they all agree to abandon children on the doorstep.

Having attracted said custom, the average neighborhood pub sets about withdrawing all services— i.e., warm drinks, no selection, no ice, no hot drinks, no acceptable food, nowhere to sit, and unspeakable wallpaper. This makes patrons feel right at home; and they get on with the serious business of doing what they do best in pubs. Being British.

DOUBLE RASPBERRY RIPPLE TO GO

———————— A M E R I - T H I N K ————————

Americans, for all their affluence and the distractions it can bring, know what really counts. ICE CREAM. More than allegiance to the flag, or a national newspaper, or Johnny Carson, or the microchip, it's mocha-chip (and peppermint crunch) that binds the nation together. Fail to appreciate this, and you've missed out on the quintessence of Ameri-culture. Ice cream is the Great Leveler . . . the Yank version of pubs. It is the fixed point in an otherwise mobile society, guaranteed to give pleasure to all. Americans will drive one hundred miles for the ultimate cone. Don't ask why. Debates about the MX missile are taken no more seriously than where you can find the best coffee flavor in Los

Angeles. It's the American way of saying that, at bottom, stripped bare of affectation, they know what life is about—and you can always appeal to them successfully on that level. Understand this, and you've gone a long way to zeroing in on Amerithink. So, grab your "I ♥ NY" T-shirt and your L.A. address book and prepare for fun. Don't worry about a thing. If you can't get to grips with the Great American Dream, you can fall back on the Great American Cream. Mocha-chip is nice.

FOR THE BEST IN PAPERBACKS, LOOK FOR THE 🐧

In every corner of the world, on every subject under the sun, Penguin represents quality and variety—the very best in publishing today.

For complete information about books available from Penguin—including Pelicans, Puffins, Peregrines, and Penguin Classics—and how to order them, write to us at the appropriate address below. Please note that for copyright reasons the selection of books varies from country to country.

In the United Kingdom: For a complete list of books available from Penguin in the U.K., please write to *Dept E.P., Penguin Books Ltd, Harmondsworth, Middlesex, UB7 0DA.*

In the United States: For a complete list of books available from Penguin in the U.S., please write to *Dept BA, Penguin,* Box 120, Bergenfield, New Jersey 07621-0120.

In Canada: For a complete list of books available from Penguin in Canada, please write to *Penguin Books Canada Ltd, 10 Alcorn Avenue, Suite 300, Toronto, Ontario, Canada M4V 3B2.*

In Australia: For a complete list of books available from Penguin in Australia, please write to the *Marketing Department, Penguin Books Ltd, P.O. Box 257, Ringwood, Victoria 3134.*

In New Zealand: For a complete list of books available from Penguin in New Zealand, please write to the *Marketing Department, Penguin Books (NZ) Ltd, Private Bag, Takapuna, Auckland 9.*

In India: For a complete list of books available from Penguin, please write to *Penguin Overseas Ltd, 706 Eros Apartments, 56 Nehru Place, New Delhi, 110019.*

In Holland: For a complete list of books available from Penguin in Holland, please write to *Penguin Books Nederland B.V., Postbus 195, NL-1380AD Weesp, Netherlands.*

In Germany: For a complete list of books available from Penguin, please write to *Penguin Books Ltd, Friedrichstrasse 10-12, D-6000 Frankfurt Main I, Federal Republic of Germany.*

In Spain: For a complete list of books available from Penguin in Spain, please write to *Longman, Penguin España, Calle San Nicolas 15, E-28013 Madrid, Spain.*

In Japan: For a complete list of books available from Penguin in Japan, please write to *Longman Penguin Japan Co Ltd, Yamaguchi Building, 2-12-9 Kanda Jimbocho, Chiyoda-Ku, Tokyo 101, Japan.*